CW00401289

THE BLUE AND WHITES

A Concise Post-War History of Blackburn Rovers

DEAN HAYES

The Parrs Wood Press
<u>MANCHESTER</u>

First Published 2000

THE PARRS WOOD PRESS
St Wilfrid's Enterprise Centre
Royce Road, Manchester, M15 5BJ
www.parrswoodpress.com

ISBN: 1 903158 13 3

Cover design by Glenn B. Fleming

This book was produced by Andrew Searle and Bob Wells of The Parrs Wood Press and Printed in Great Britain by:

MFP Design & Print
Longford Trading Estate
Thomas Street
Stretford
Manchester M32 0JT

CONTENTS

The Blue and Whites

ACKNOWLEDGEMENTS

I would like to express my grateful thanks to the following organisations who helped in the compilation of this book: Blackburn Rovers Football Club, the Football League Ltd., the Association of Football Statisticians, Blackburn Reference Library and the Harris Library. Many thanks, too, to the Lanacshire Evening Post for providing most of the photographs in this book. I would like to express my gratitude to Andy Searle of The Parrs Wood Press for supporting the series of concise post-war histories of north west football clubs.

ABOUT THE AUTHOR

Dean Hayes is an experienced and prolific freelance sports writer specialising in football and cricket. He was educated at Hayward Grammar School, Bolton and West Midlands College of Physical Education and before taking up writing full-time four years ago, he was a primary school headmaster. Having played as a goalkeeper in the Lancashire Amateur League, he now concentrates solely on the summer sport. This former cricket professional, now playing as an amateur, has taken over 2,000 wickets in League Cricket. Dean is married with a son and two step-cildren.

The Blue and Whites

A
CONCISE
POST-WAR HISTORY
OF
BLACKBURN ROVERS

BOB CROMPTON, the greatest figure in Blackburn Rovers' history, led the club to the Second Division Championship in 1938-39 but the outbreak of the Second World War prevented him from re-establishing Rovers in the top flight. He did take the club to the 1940 War Cup Final but Rovers suffered a devastating blow in March 1941 when Crompton collapsed and died within hours of supervising a match against Burnley.

As peace returned, former Arsenal and England full-back Eddie Hapgood was appointed manager, bringing his old colleague at Highbury, Horace Cope, with him as trainer. During the 1945-46 season, Rovers had conceded 111 goals, so it came as no surprise when Hapgood signed George Marks, a wartime international goalkeeper. His only other signing of note was former Newcastle United and Manchester United centre-forward Jack Smith.

After losing 3-1 at Portsmouth on the opening day of the 1946-47 season, Rovers enjoyed three successive victories, including a 3-1 win at Arsenal and a 4-1 home defeat of Everton when Jack Smith netted the club's first post-war hat-trick, but unfortunately these results were followed by five successive defeats. Hampered by injuries to Crook, Butt and Glaister, Hapgood tried to turn things round by introducing a number of younger players. Sadly, this made little impact on the results and with some of the established players becoming unsettled after being played out of position, it was clear that Hapgood had a relegation battle on his hands. At the turn of the year, full-back Walter Crook asked to be placed on the transfer list and with Hapgood unable to find a winning combination, Rovers' directors decided to enter the transfer market in an attempt to stave off the threat of relegation. However, the manager's and director's choice of targets differed and though Rovers splashed out a club record fee of £10,000 to bring Hibernian centre-forward Jock Weir to Ewood Park along with Jackie Oates from Queen of the South and Alec Venters from Third Lanark, results didn't improve. Relations between Hapgood and the board had become so difficult that in February 1947, the former Arsenal defender resigned his post.

Horace Cope took charge until Will Scott, the Preston North End secretary and former trainer, was appointed manager in early May 1947. Five points were taken from the final four games of the season and Rovers ended the campaign 17th in the First Division.

BOBBY LANGTON

Bobby Langton was a promising teenager who signed for Blackburn Rovers for just £50 from Southport League side Burscough Victoria in 1937. Within twelve months of his arrival at Ewood Park, he had established himself in the Rovers' first team and in the club's promotion-winning campaign of 1938-39 scored 14 goals in 37 appearances.

During the war he was an infantryman in India and represented the army in practically every game they played during his service. He appeared in the 1940 War Cup Final when Rovers lost 1-0 to West Ham United. The end of the war saw him restored to the Blackburn side and in September 1946 he won his first cap for England against Northern Ireland. Blackburn's fortunes began to wane and in August 1949 he was transferred to Preston North End for £16,000. In the same month he netted a goal after only seven seconds from the kick-off against Manchester City. In November 1949 Langton was on his way to Bolton Wanderers for what was then a club record fee of £20,000.

At Bolton he became a regular in the number eleven shirt until 1953, when he was placed on the transfer list at his own request. He remained long enough to play in the famous 1953 FA Cup Final against Blackpool before in September of that year returning to play at Ewood Park.

Although his speed had diminished somewhat in his second spell at Blackburn, he added a great deal of guile and cunning to his play. He had scored 58 goals in 230 League and Cup games for Rovers when he left to play in Ireland with Ards. Langton then entered non-League football with Kidderminster Harriers before playing for Wisbech Town and Colwyn Bay.

In 1962 he became trainer-coach at King's Lynn and a year later took over a similar position at Wisbech. Five years later he returned to his roots, becoming manager of Burscough Rangers.

The 1947-48 season was only three games old - all defeats - when it was announced that Scott had been ordered to take a complete rest by his doctor. The club's playing affairs were put in the hands of the former England international Jack Bruton and though Scott returned within a matter of weeks, the directors decided to appoint Bruton on a permanent basis. His immediate aim was to avoid relegation but after just one win in the last ten games of the season - a 4-0 home defeat of Sheffield United in which Leslie Graham scored a hat-trick, Rovers were sent tumbling into the Second Division.

During the close season, Bruton planned for a quick return to the top flight. Bill Eckersley, a young lorry driver from Southport, who had made his debut in the final game of the previous season, kept his place in

BILL ECKERSLEY

Bill Eckersley was an ex-lorry driver from Southport who might never have played for Blackburn Rovers if they hadn't been a man short for an 'A' team fixture at Feniscowles. He got to play in borrowed boots with string for shoelaces and only a couple of studs on each boot!

In the last game of the 1947-48 season, the Rovers, who were already doomed to relegation, gave him his first-team chance. Over the course of the next few seasons he matured into the club's most outstanding player after quickly establishing himself in the first team.

He was selected as Alf Ramsey's regular partner in the England team, winning 17 full caps between 1950 and 1953. Perhaps he should have had more, for he was extremely tenacious, very fit and quick.

Despite his success on the international scene, club honours eluded him. A number of promotion near-misses and two FA Cup semi-finals were all that were achieved during his prime. Unfortunately his career was coming to an end when promotion was finally achieved in 1957-58. He was plagued by injuries and missed the 1959-60 FA Cup run. During his final two seasons he only made a handful of appearances, taking his tally of goals to 21 in 432 League and Cup games. He retired in 1961 and a crowd of 21,000 turned up to pay him an emotional farewell at Ewood in his testimonial.

Unfortunately his life outside the game wasn't kind to him and a confectionary business he ran near Ewood wasn't a success. He returned to driving during his later days before he died at the tragically early age of 54. The ashes of this player of limitless talent were scattered on the Ewood turf by his sons Billy and Stephen in an emotional ceremony before a first-team game.

4

the side for the opening game of the 1948-49 campaign, a 3-0 defeat at Southampton. New signings included winger Jackie Wharton from Manchester City, who had replaced Bobby Langton, the England international joining Preston North End, and Dennis Westcott, the Wolverhampton Wanderers' centre-forward who had scored 124 goals in 144 League and Cup games for the Molineux club, 215 in 220 games if you include the war years! Westcott certainly lived up to his reputation, scoring 21 goals in 36 league games including doubles in the wins over Barnsley (Home 5-3) Luton Town (Home 4-1) Plymouth Argyle (Home 2-1) Lincoln City (Home 7-1) and Leicester City (Home 2-0). However, Rovers only managed 14th place in the Second Division and in May 1949, the services of both Bruton and Horace Cope were dispensed with.

Within a month of Bruton's departure, the Blackburn board appointed the former Grimsby Town and England international Jackie Bestall as his replacement. Assisted on the coaching staff by two former Ewood favourites, Jock Weddle and Jock Wightman, Bestall set about reviving Rovers' fortunes. However, he was faced with an immediate problem when long-serving Bob Pryde, who appeared in 345 games either side of the Second World War, decided to become the player-manager of Wigan Athletic.

Dennis Westcott continued to find the net on a regular basis in 1949-50, scoring hat-tricks in the wins over Brentford (Home 4-1) and Barnsley (Home 4-0) but in February 1950, after scoring 37 goals in 66 games, he was surprisingly allowed to leave Ewood Park and join Manchester City. The team finished in 16th position, whilst Liverpool ended their interest in the FA Cup with a third round replay win.

Bestall signed a number of youngsters, including future England internationals Ronnie Clayton and Bryan Douglas, with the former being given his league debut on the final day of the 1950-51 season in a 2-1 home win over Queen's Park Rangers. Rovers had started the campaign in great style, winning their opening three matches with Eddie Crossan and Les Graham beginning to form a promising strike force. At the turn of the year, Rovers won five and drew one one of their first six matches, form that was to see them maintain a place on the fringe of the promotion pack. However, after injuries to Crossan and Graham, Rovers found goals hard to come by with the final seven games of the season producing just four goals. The goal drought saw Rovers end the campaign in sixth place.

After being beaten 5-1 at home by Sheffield United on the opening day of the 1951-52 season, Rovers drew two and lost seven of their opening nine matches, ending September firmly rooted to the foot of the Second Division. Bestall went in urgent need of reinforcements, signing Bolton Wanderers' 'keeper Reg Elvy, Willie Carr, a rugged centre-half from Airdrieonians, and Eddie Quigley, once the country's most expensive player, from Preston North End. Eventually, after 12 defeats in the opening 16 league matches, the new signings began to blend together and from 29 December 1951 to 16 February 1952, Rovers won seven consecutive league games, including a 4-2 defeat of Queen's Park Rangers when Bill Eckersley scored twice from the penalty-spot, eventually ending the season in 14th place.

This improvement in form came just in time for the start of the club's FA Cup campaign. After drawing 2-2 at Nottingham Forest in the third round, Rovers won 2-0 at Ewood Park with Bill Holmes scoring in both games. Hull City were beaten by the same scoreline in round four whilst a Bill Eckersley penalty was enough to defeat West Bromwich Albion in the fifth round. In the quarter-final, Rovers were drawn at home to arch rivals Burnley. A crowd of 52,920 saw goals from Nightingale, Holmes and Glover defeat the Clarets 3-1. The semi-final saw Rovers paired with First Division high flyers Newcastle United at Hillsborough. After weathering a lot of early pressure from the Magpies, Rovers got back into the game but had to settle for a goalless draw. The replay was held at Elland Road, where an injury-hit Rovers conceded an early goal to George Robledo before Eddie Quigley levelled things up with a spectacular left-foot volley. Rovers pressed forward in search of the winner, but in a rare breakaway Newcastle were awarded a penalty when Jackie Campbell fisted the ball over the bar after 'keeper Reg Elvy had been impeded in going for a cross. Bobby Mitchell sent Elvy the wrong way from the spot to send the Magpies through to the Wembley final.

Hopes were high for the 1952-53 season and though Rovers lost 4-1 at Lincoln City following a 2-1 win at Nottingham Forest on the opening day of the season, a hat-trick from Bill Holmes helped the Ewood Park club beat Everton 3-1. However, the goals then began to dry up and in November 1952, Bestall signed Tommy Briggs and Bill Smith from

Birmingham City, though the former suffered a knee injury after scoring nine goals in 17 games. Rovers ended the season in ninth place, whilst in the FA Cup the exploits of the previous season were not continued as Rovers went out in the third round, 6-1 at Luton Town. The Hatters also won 6-0 at Kenilworth Road in the league meeting! Following rumours of disputes between the manager and the players, the Rovers board announced that Bestall had decided that a parting of the ways would be in the best interest of both parties.

The directors turned to Johnny Carey, who had enjoyed a hugely successful career with Manchester United and had been capped by both the Republic of Ireland and Northern Ireland. Carey captained United to victory in the 1948 FA Cup Final and, twelve months later, was named Footballer of the Year. One of the game's true gentlemen, Carey decided

EDDIE CROSSAN

The mercurial Eddie Crossan played his early football for Glentoran but was playing for Derry City when Blackburn Rovers paid £3,000 for his services in November 1947. He made his Rovers debut in a 4-3 home win over Sunderland in January 1948 and soon became a great favourite with the Ewood Park faithful.

Possessing great close control, he was able to dazzle his opponents with his silky skills, but he was also unpredicatble and it was this that prevented him from becoming one of the greatest players of his era.

Though not a prolific goalscorer, often missing the simplest of chances, the goals that he did score were often quite memorable. His best season in terms of goals scored was 1954-55 when he netted 18 times, including a hat-trick in a 4-1 home win over Rotherham United.

Whilst with Rovers, Crossan won three full caps for Northern Ireland but in the summer of 1957, after scoring 74 goals in 302 League and Cup games, he left Ewood Park to join Tranmere Rovers. He spent just one season at Prenton Park before returning to his native Ireland to play for Cork Hibernians.

His younger brother Johnny Crossan was less talented but a more consistent inside-forward who won 23 caps for Ireland in a career that included spells with Standard Liege, Sunderland, Manchester City and Middlesbrough.

EDDIE QUIGLEY

In December 1949, Eddie Quigley became the most expensive foot-baller in Britain when he joined Preston North End from Sheffield Wednesday for £26,000.

He joined Blackburn Rovers in November 1951 and scored the only goal of the game on his debut against Birmingham City. As a player, his movements were totally deceptive, for his speed of thought and precise passing made him a constant threat to the opposition defences.

Under Johnny Carey's attacking philosphy, Quigley's goalscoring flourished, his long-range shooting having both accuracy and power. His best season in terms of goals scored was 1954-55, when his total of 28 goals in 40 league games included hat-tricks in the games against Middlesbrough (Home 9-0) and Notts County (Home 4-5).

He had scored 95 goals in 166 League and Cup games for Rovers when in August 1956 he left Ewood Park and returned to his home-town club Bury for a short spell before entering non-League football as manager of Mossley. After returning to Gigg Lane as coach, he managed Stockport County before joining Blackburn Rovers as assi-atant-manager in November 1966.

Although only assistant-manager, Quigley had insisted that he be in sole charge of coaching throughout the club. A master tactician, he soon began to show his influence on Jack Marshall's team. Following Marshall's resignation in February 1967, Quigley was appointed care-taker manager, a position that became permanent some two months later. Though he kept Rovers in the promotion hunt for the next two seasons, the club didn't mount a serious challenge and in October 1970, with the club languishing at the foot of the Second Division, he exchanged duties with Johnny Carey, who was then the club's admin-istrative manager. Though he was put in charge of scouting, he, along with Carey, was sacked after the club's relegation to the Third Division.

He found employment with Rovers a third time in 1979 when Howard Kendall appointed him chief scout, a position he held until Kendall's departure in 1981, thus ending an association which on and off lasted almost thirty years.

to take charge of the first team coaching, which meant there was no room for the former FA Cup winning captain Harry Healless on the staff.

Rovers began the 1953-54 season in fine style, winning 4-1 at Rotherham United on the opening day of the campaign and by the same scoreline two games later at Brentford. In this latter match, Tommy Briggs scored his first hat-trick for the club. However, two days after the Griffin Park encounter, Rovers travelled to Lincoln City and lost 8-0! This prompted Carey to re-sign former favourite Bobby Langton from Preston North End and he provided the guile and craft which helped Briggs to score 32 goals in 41 games, the best since Ted Harper netted 35 goals in 1926-27. Briggs scored four in the return game with Lincoln City as Rovers gained revenge with a 6-0 win and then netted his third hat-trick of the campaign in the following match as Rovers won 5-0 at Notts County. After beating Swansea Town 1-0 in the final game of the season, courtesy of an Eddie Quigley goal, Rovers found themselves in second place in Division Two. Unfortunately, Everton, who were third, one point behind the Ewood Park club, had one more game to play and that was against already relegated Oldham Athletic. Despite the unlikelihood of a Latics victory, Rovers fans swelled the gate to 30,072, but it didn't stop Everton from winning 4-0 to leapfrog over the Rovers and win promotion!

In 1954-55, Rovers achieved an even greater number of individual records but still fell short of the main aim, promotion to the First Division. After losing 5-1 at Fulham on the opening day of the season, Rovers netted 14 goals in the next three games as West Ham United were beaten 5-2 at both Ewood and Upton Park and Swansea Town were defeated 4-1. On 6 November 1954, Rovers recorded their biggest-ever victory in the Football League when they beat Middlesbrough 9-0 with both Eddie Quigley and Frank Mooney netting hat-tricks. Surprisingly, one of the club's most prolific goalscorers, Tommy Briggs, failed to get on the scoresheet. There were some remarkable results at the turn of the year with Doncaster Rovers on the wrong end of a 7-0 scoreline and Eddie Quigley netting a hat-trick in a 5-4 defeat at Notts County. When Bristol Rovers visited Ewood Park on 5 February 1955, Tommy Briggs more than made up for not scoring in the defeat of Middlesbrough by rewriting the record books. The popular striker scored seven goals in succession as the then Eastville club were beaten 8-3. The first game of the season in which

9

RONNIE CLAYTON

Ronnie Clayton joined the Rovers in 1949, making his league debut at the age of 16 in the final game of the 1950-51 season, a 2-1 win over Queen's Park Rangers. His early promise led the Blackburn manager Jackie Bestall to predict an England future for the talented youngster.

Clayton had natural leadership qualities which showed early in his career. In September 1955 he won his first Under-23 cap and a month later he appeared for the England 'B' team. In November of that year he completed the international sequence when he made his debut for the full England team.

He was a tremendous driving force in Blackburn's promotion back to the First Division in 1957-58. Clayton was an energetic wing-half, strong in the tackle and a brilliant timer of the ball in the air. He also liked to power forward and instigate attacking moves.

He appeared in the final stages of the 1958 World Cup in Sweden and succeeded Billy Wright as captain for the last five of his 35 England appearances. He then lost favour with the England selectors and, surprisingly, didn't play again for his country after 1960.

He continued to give good service to Blackburn and led them to Wembley in 1960, only for them to lose 3-0 to Wolverhampton Wanderers. Remaining loyal to what many would class an unfashionable club, Ronnie Clayton experienced the highs and lows but always maintained the same level of enthusiasm and endeavour. As age began to slow down his legs, he moved to play at the heart of the defence where he became a very accomplished centre-back. It was Clayton's masterful reading of the game that provided the solid defensive platform for the team.

He left Ewood at the end of the 1968-69 season, having scored 16 goals in 665 League and Cup games, to become player-manager at Morecambe. He later returned to north-east Lancashire to play for Great Harwood. Throughout a career that spanned 19 seasons, Ronnie Clayton remained one of football's finest ambassadors. He was, without doubt, one of the greatest players ever to wear the Rovers' colours.

The Blue and Whites

Rovers failed to score saw them beaten 2-0 by Swansea Town in the the third round of the FA Cup, but it was 5 March before Rovers failed to find the net in the league, when Nottingham Forest won 1-0 at Ewood Park. Two weeks later, Eddie Quigley scored the opening goal in a 2-0 home win over Stoke City to register the club's 100th goal of the season. However, it was this month which brought a slump in Rovers' form, thus ending the club's promotion dream, and after taking just two points from the last four games of the season, the Ewood Park club had to settle for sixth place. Despite scoring 114 goals, the Rovers' defence conceded 79 and that was certainly not promotion form!

Despite a disappointing start to the 1955-56 season, Rovers rallied and over the autumn months, six wins in eight matches, including a 7-1 rout of Port Vale in which Eddie Crossan scored a hat-trick, moved them on to the fringe of the promotion places. Unfortunately, in the month of December, Rovers took just one point - a 2-2 draw against Sheffield Wednesday - and this plunged the club into relegation trouble. However, between 31 December 1955 and 2 April 1956, Rovers collected 22 points out of a possible 28 and climbed from 18th to third place in Division Two. Unfortunately though, the damage had been done and even three wins over Easter failed to push Rovers into the promotion frame, the club ending the campaign in fourth place. That season, Rovers reached the fifth round of the FA Cup after wins over Northampton Town (Away 2-1) and Barnsley (Away 1-0) but lost 3-2 to West Ham United in a replay at Ewood Park, a team Rovers had done the 'double' over in the league.

During the close season, Reg Elvy, Eddie Quigley and Bobby Langton left Ewood Park to be replaced by Harry Leyland, Ally MacLeod and Roy Vernon, who had worked his way up through the ranks. Another youngster, Peter Dobing, made his debut in November 1956 whilst Carey signed centre-half Matt Woods from Everton.

Rovers didn't make the best of starts to the 1956-57 season, losing 5-1 at Swansea Town on the opening day of the campaign. They bounced back two days latr with a 3-1 win at West Ham United but then went down 4-3 to Lincoln City in their first game at Ewood Park. Results up until Christmas were mixed, the games against Fulham over the festive period being no different. On Christmas Day, Rovers beat the Cottagers 2-0 whilst on Boxing Day, Fulham thrashed Blackburn 7-2 with youngster Peter

TOMMY BRIGGS

Tommy Briggs was a centre-forward in the traditional mould, a man who relied upon others to create chances which he converted with great consistency. Though he was not the most skilful of players, the power of his heading, running and shooting made him a feared opponent.

Chesterfield-born Briggs was a butcher by trade and played junior football in the Doncaster area. During the war years he served in the Royal Navy and being stationed in Plymouth, he 'guested' for Argyle. In May 1947 he arrived on trial at Grimsby Town and over the next four seasons he scored 87 goals in 135 appearances for the Mariners. In 1949-50 he not only topped Grimsby's scoring charts but was also top marksman in the Football League with 36 goals, and in January of that season was capped by the England 'B' team.

Following his move to Coventry City for £20,000 in January 1951 he was unable to settle and early the following season he joined Birmingham City. After a good first season at St Andrew's, he was surprisingly allowed to leave and joined Blackburn Rovers for a fee of £15,000.

Tommy Briggs was hugely popular with the Ewood faithful and in each of four successive seasons topped thirty league goals. In 1953-54, his total of 32 goals included four in the 6-0 defeat of Lincoln City and hat-tricks against Brentford (Away 4-1) and Notts County (Away 5-0). In 1954-55 he was again the League's leading goalscorer with 33 goals, including seven in succession in the 8-3 win over Bristol Rovers.

The 1957-58 season brought an end to his Ewood career when he lost form and doubts were raised about his fitness. Briggs, who had scored 143 goals in 204 League and Cup games, was allowed to return to Grimsby and later moved to Glentoran as player-manager.

Although Simon Garner broke Tommy Briggs' league aggregate scoring record in terms of goals per game, he remains the most prolific league scorer in the club's modern history.

Dobing grabbing both Rovers' goals. However, the club's next defeat wasn't until 4 April 1957, Rovers' embarking on a 13-match unbeaten run. On 6 April, Rovers not only lost 2-1 at Middlesbrough but wing-half Ken

Clayton suffered a broken leg which virtually ended his first-class career, for he only made three more appearances for the club. Rovers finished the season in fourth place, which was a remarkable achievement considering the lack of experience in the team.

Despite a poor start to the 1957-58 season, in which Rovers won just one of their opening five matches, hopes were still high amongst the Ewood Park faithful that the club would win promotion. Up until the turn of the year, results were mixed - Welsh clubs Swansea Town and Cardiff City were both beaten 4-0 but Rovers went down 5-1 at Leyton Orient. On 28 December 1957, Rovers beat Notts County 3-0 with Ally MacLeod netting a hat-trick after which they lost just two of their remaining 17 league games. The only weak-link in the Blackburn side was at centre-forward where the ageing Tommy Briggs had suffered a loss of form. With 11 games to play, manager Johnny Carey signed the veteran Leyton Orient centre-forward Tommy Johnston. He scored twice on his debut in a 3-0 home win over Grimsby Town and ended the campaign with seven goals in his 11 games. Rovers won eight and drew one of Johnston's first ten matches, including a 4-1 win over his former club in a game in which Roy Vernon scored his first hat-trick for the Rovers. Bryan Douglas had netted a hat-trick in a 5-1 win at Doncaster Rovers whilst Peter Dobing, who topped the scoring charts with 20 goals in 34 league games, scored four in the 5-0 home defeat of Bristol City.

After ending Fulham's promotion ambitions on the penultimate day of the season, Rovers travelled to Charlton Athletic on the final day of the campaign knowing that anything less than a win would send the Addicks into the First Division. Both Charlton and West Ham United had 55 points whilst Rovers were a point behind with an inferior goal average.

A crowd of 56,435 were crammed into The Valley and saw the home side take an early lead before missing a golden opportunity to go further ahead. Despite Rovers' nervous start, they gradually got back into the game and equalised through Peter Dobing, who increased their lead after latching on to a beautiful long pass from Bill Eckersley before shooting past Duff in the Charlton goal. Just before half-time, Roy Vernon shot home from fully 25 yards to give Rovers a 3-1 lead at the interval. On 65 minutes, Tommy Johnston was fouled in the penalty area and Bryan Douglas scored from the spot to give Rovers what seemed an unassailable 4-1 lead.

However, Charlton were not prepared to lie down and die and pulled two goals back, the second a penalty after Matt Woods' clumsy challenge on Stuart Leary. The big defender, along with 'keeper Harry Leyland, more than made amends in the final few minutes to keep Charlton at bay and thus ensure promotion to the First Division for Rovers.

The top of Division Two read as follows:

	P.	W.	D.	L.	F.	A.	Pts
West Ham United	42	23	11	8	101	54	57
Blackburn Rovers	42	22	12	8	93	57	56
Charlton Athletic	42	24	7	11	107	69	55

In that season's FA Cup competition, Rovers beat Rotherham United 4-1 at Millmoor in the third round with Peter Dobing netting a hat-trick. The England Under-23 international was on target again in the fourth round as Rovers beat First Division Everton 2-1 at Goodison Park. After playing out a goalless draw at Cardiff City in round five, goals by McGrath and Douglas helped Rovers beat the Bluebirds 2-1 in the replay. In the quarter-finals, Rovers were drawn at home to Liverpool. A crowd of 51,000 saw goals by Clayton and MacLeod help defeat the Anfield side 2-1. Rovers' opponents in the semi-final at Maine Road were Bolton Wanderers. The Burnden Park club were without the legendary Nat Lofthouse, whilst Rovers' recent signing Tom Johnston was ineleigible for the tie. Playing in an unfamiliar black and white striped kit, Rovers took the lead in the first-half through Peter Dobing but then two goals from Ralph Gubbins, who was deputising for the injured Lofthouse, sent Rovers crashing out of the competition.

Rovers' manager Johnny Carey decided to stand by the players that had taken the club into the First Division and, after the first three games of the 1958-59 campaign, the decision looked to be well founded as Newcastle United (Away 5-1), Leicester City (Home 5-0) and Tottenham Hotspur (Home 5-0) were all well beaten. However, then came the news that Carey was about to leave Ewood Park and take over the reins at struggling Everton. The amiable Irishman agreed to delay his departure until the club had found a replacement. His successor was Luton Town manager Dally Duncan. Unfortunately, September and October saw Rovers pick up just

15

BRYAN DOUGLAS

Practically living on the doorstep of Ewood Park, Bryan Douglas joined his home-town team as a groundstaff boy in 1952 after he had had much success with Blackburn Schoolboys.

Unfortunately for Bryan and Blackburn, National Service disrupted his early career and he did not make his first team debut until September 1954 in a 3-1 defeat at Notts County. During those early days in the team he was often criticised for being over-elaborate and too selfish. Deceptively frail-looking, he was later to confound those critics and become one of England's greatest post-war footballers.

During the club's promotion-winning season of 1957-58, Douglas made his England debut against Wales, wearing Stanley Matthews' number seven shirt. Considering that Douglas played in the era of Finney, Matthews, Charlton, Haynes and Greaves, he did well to play for his country so often. In fact, he won 36 caps and scored 11 goals - an excellent return for a winger.

Blackburn preferred to use him as a scheming inside-forward. He had the most perfect close control it is possible to see. His shuffling feet carved up opposing defences for more than a decade, during which he made a succession of forwards - notably Fred Pickering and Andy McEvoy - into frequent goalscorers. On a muddy Upton Park pitch on Boxing Day 1963, he was the executioner-in-chief as Pickering and McEvoy both claimed hat-tricks as Rovers beat West Ham 8-2.

Douglas was a member of the Blackburn side that reached the FA Cup Final in 1960 and played in all four of England's games in the 1962 World Cup Finals in Chile. A cartilage operation coupled with other injuries meant that he missed most of Blackburn's struggle against relegation in 1965-66.

Sadly, his final years at Ewood were dogged by injury and at the end of the 1968-69 season, after which he had scored 111 goals in 503 League and Cup games, he left Ewood Park and spent a couple of seasons playing non-League football for Great Harwood with Ronnie Clayton and Roy Vernon.

three points from eight matches and suffer a couple of heavy defeats - Manchester United (Away 1-6) and West Ham United (Away 3-6). After that defeat at Upton Park, Rovers lost just two of the 13 matches to the turn of the year. In that sequence, Tom Johnston netted a hat-trick in a 3-0 home win over Newcastle United but in February 1959, the veteran striker was allowed to rejoin Leyton Orient for £8,000, having scored 22 goals in 38 games. He was replaced by Derek Dougan, who had long been admired by the Ewood Park officials, but even so his £10,000 transfer from Portsmouth surprised the majority of Rovers' fans.

Blackburn ended the season in a highly creditable tenth position but the highlight of the campaign was the performance of the club's youngsters, who reached the final of the FA Youth Cup where they beat West Ham United over two legs. The side contained a number of promising players including Mike England, Keith Newton and Fred Pickering.

The first half of the 1959-60 season saw the club hit by one of the worst epidemics of illness and injury that could ever be remembered at Ewood Park. Yet Rovers won four and drew one of their opening five fixtures before results began to become much more erratic. Though victories were in short supply, Derek Dougan scored four times in a 6-2 home win over West Ham United. Former manager Johnny Carey returned to Ewood Park to sign Welsh international inside-forward Roy Vernon for a club record fee of £27,000. Before leaving Rovers, Vernon, who had scored twice in an FA Cup third round replay win over Sunderland, provided the pass for Mick McGrath to score a last minute equaliser against Blackpool in the fourth round. In the replay, two goals by Dobing and another by Dougan gave Rovers a comfortable 3-0 win over the Seasiders. In the fifth round, Louis Bimpson netted twice in a 3-1 win over Spurs at White Hart Lane, yet in the league the club were having great difficulty in finding the net. In the quarter-finals, Rovers met arch rivals Burnley at Turf Moor but looked to be going out of the competition as they trailed 3-0 with just 17 minutes remaining. A harmless looking shot by Peter Dobing struck Alex Elder on the boot and flew up on to his hand. Unbelievably the referee pointed to the penalty-spot and Bryan Douglas coolly slotted the ball home. Three minutes later, Dobing reduced the arrears with a powerfully-struck 25-yard drive. Four minutes from the end, Mick McGrath sliced a shot past Adam Blacklaw to give Rovers an unexpected replay. The game at Ewood Park attracted a crowd of 53,839 and though Rovers dominated proceedings they couldn't turn their superiority into goals. The game went to extra-time where goals from Dobing and MacLeod clinched a semi-final spot for the Ewood Park club. Their opponents at Maine Road were Sheffield Wednesday, the Owls losing 2-1 to a brace from Derek Dougan.

The final eight league games of the season brought just four points as Rovers ended the campaign in 17th place, grateful for the fact that their early season form had prevented them from being relegated.

On the journey to Wembley, where their opponents in the FA Cup

ROY VERNON

One of Ewood's 'Carey Chicks', Prestatyn-born inside-forward Roy Vernon made his league debut for Blackburn Rovers in September 1955 in a 3-3 home draw against Liverpool. By the time he had reached 19, Vernon had won full international honours, playing for Wales against Northern Ireland.

A creative player who struck a dead ball with tremendous power and great accuracy, Vernon was a member of the Welsh side that reached the quarter-finals of the 1958 World Cup Finals in Sweden. Unfortunately, he began to grow disillusioned with life at Ewood Park and in February 1960, after scoring 52 goals in 144 League and Cup games, he followed his mentor Johnny Carey to Everton for a fee of £27,000. Although he didn't realise it at the time, Vernon robbed himself of a Wembley appearance with this move.

In 1960-61 he was the Everton's top scorer with 21 goals, including a hat-trick in a 4-1 win over Arsenal on the final day of the season. In 1961-62 he was again the club's top scorer with 26 goals in 37 league appearances, including another hat-trick in an 8-3 win over Cardiff City. Appointed captain, he skippered Everton to the League Championship in 1962-63, netting another treble in the 4-1 win over Fulham, a result that clinched the title for the Blues. He scored 110 goals in 199 games for Everton before moving to Stoke City for £40,000 in March 1965.

He eventually won 32 caps for Wales and when he lost his place in the Stoke side after five productive years with the Potters, he moved to Halifax Town where he ended his league career. He returned to Lancashire in 1970 to join former Ewood team-mates Ronnie Clayton and Bryan Douglas at Great Harwood, helping to take the Northern Premier League club into the first round of the FA Cup for the first time in its history.

Final were Wolverhampton Wanderers, Derek Dougan chose to hand in a transfer request!

FA Cup Final 1960: Blackburn Rovers 0 Wolverhampton Wanderers 3

Rovers fell behind when Mick McGrath had the misfortune to deflect a Barry Stobart cross past Harry Leyland. A minute later, the game was as good as lost when Rovers' full-back Dave Whelan broke his leg in a clash with Wolves' diminutive winger Norman Deeley. Two further goals from Deeley clinched the trophy for the Molineux club in one of the most disappointing of Wembley finals.

At the end of the season, the board of directors asked Dally Duncan to resign but with the security of a long-term contract behind him, he refused. However, with the club's league form not matching that of Rovers' Cup exploits, they were left with no option but to sack him and look for a successor.

The directors chose to replace Duncan with Jack Marshall, who was manager of Rochdale, but the Spotland club wouldn't release him until they had appointed his successor. Meanwhile, the club's directors took responsibility for team selection, beginning the season with two good wins - Manchester United (Away 3-1), with Derek Dougan netting a hat-trick, and Nottingham Forest (Home 4-1).

Marshall took over after six games of the 1960-61 season but was immediateley met with selection problems with regard to the senior playing members. Early season injuries to Leyland, Bray and Eckersley, coupled with the fact that Dave Whelan was still recovering from his broken leg, left the new manager with no option but to blood some of the club's youngsters. Up until Christmas the club turned in a series of indifferent performances, including beating Fulham 5-1 and then losing 5-4 at Sheffield Wednesday the following week.

This was the first season of the newly introduced Football League Cup competition but after beating York City (Away 3-1), Swansea Town (Away 2-1) and Rochdale (Home 2-1) Rovers lost to Fourth Division Wrexham after a replay!

The club seemed to save their best performances for the FA Cup. After a goalless draw at Chesterfield in the third round, Rovers saw off the

ALLY MacLEOD

A former Scottish schoolboy international, Ally MacLeod played his early football with Third Lanark and St Mirren before he became Johnny Carey's costliest signing when he arrived at Ewood Park in the summer of 1956.

Tall, blond and rather clumsy, MacLeod was a speedy winger with an eye for goal. The Rovers faithful soon took to him and nicknamed him 'Noddy' because of a peculiar nodding motion he made with his head when running.

During the club's promotion-winning season of 1957-58, MacLeod scored 17 goals in 38 games, including a hat-trick in a 3-0 home win over Notts County. MacLeod, who also won an FA Cup runners-up medal in 1960, was a regular on the Blackburn left flank for five seasons, but in 1961, after scoring 51 goals in 218 League and Cup games, he returned to his native Scotland to play for Hibernian.

In 1963 he rejoined Third Lanark but two years later was appointed player-coach of Ayr United. Within a few months of his arrival at Somerset Park, he accepted the position of manager.

He spent ten seasons in charge of Ayr before accepting the manager's job at Aberdeen, one of Scotland's leading clubs of the day. The success he achieved at Pittodrie led to him being appointed as manager of the national side.

He took Scotland to the 1978 World Cup Finals in Argentina but unfortunately fate treated him cruelly. On his return home, Ayr offered him the chance to become their manager, and though shortly after taking up the appointment he was offered the opportunity to manage Blackburn Rovers following Jim Iley's departure, he decided to stay in Scotland and stay loyal to Ayr United. MacLeod later managed Motherwell and Airdrie before returning to Ayr United for a third term of office.

Spireites 3-0 in the replay to set up a fourth round tie with Bolton Wanderers. This too went to a replay after a gripping 3-3 draw at Burnden Park where Ally MacLeod scored two of Rovers' goals. Four days later, a crowd of 31,000 packed into Ewood Park to witness probably the club's best display of the season. Two goals apiece from Dobing and Douglas gave Rovers a 4-0 win and a place in the fifth round at Sheffield United.

Unfortunately, the Blades won 2-1 to end any hopes the club had of returning to Wembley.

Though the club finished eighth in the First Division, the close season brought the expected departures of Peter Dobing and Derek Dougan, who joined Manchester City and Aston Villa respectively, whilst Ally

PETER DOBING

The son of a former Salford Rugby League player, Peter Dobing began his first-class career with Blackburn Rovers after manager Johnny Carey brought him to Ewood Park in the face of stiff competition from a number of top clubs. He played in the club's 'A' team as a 16-year-old and, after signing professional forms on his 17th birthday, was promoted to the club's Central League side.

He made his league debut for Rovers in a 3-0 defeat at Bristol City in September 1956 and kept his place in the side as Rovers finished fourth in Division Two.

When Rovers won promotion to the First Division in 1957-58, Dobing was the club's leading scorer with 20 goals in 34 games, including four in the 5-0 defeat of Bristol City. He also netted five goals in that season's FA Cup competition, including a hat-trick in a 4-1 win at Rotherham United. Dobing headed Rovers' scoring charts again in 1958-59 with 24 goals in the top flight, including another hat-trick in a 4-2 win over Arsenal. Dobing continued to be the club's leading scorer over the next couple of seasons and netted five goals in Rovers' run to the FA Cup Final in 1960.

Although he won honours at Football League and Under-23 levels, he was unable to break into the England senior team.

He had scored 104 goals in 205 games for Rovers when in July 1961, Manchester City paid £37,500 for his services.

Unable to settle at Maine Road, Dobing moved to Stoke City to strengthen a Potters' side that had just won promotion to the First Division. He went on to make 372 first team appearances in ten seasons at the Victoria Ground. Undoubtedly, his proudest day was when he led Stoke to victory in the 1972 Football League Cup Final against Chelsea.

A keen cricketer, he came on as 12th man for Lancashire in a Roses match.

MATT WOODS

Though he was christened Maurice, he was known as Matt to everyone. He moved from junior football to become an amateur with Everton in 1947, signing professional forms two years later. Whilst in the army, he played football with the Western Command but on his return to Goodison Park he found he couldn't break into the first team.

In November 1956, Johnny Carey paid £6,000 to bring Woods to Ewood Park and he made his debut in a 1-0 home win over Middlesbrough. Playing between Ronnie Clayton and Mick McGrath, Woods helped to form one of the best half-back lines in the club's history. He was ever-present in 1957-58 when the club won promotion to the First Division and won an FA Cup runners-up medal in 1960.

Although he played for the Football League, he never won full international honours. He managed to keep the highly promising Mike England out of the team but in 1963, after playing in 307 League and Cup games, he decided to retire from first-class football and emigrated to Australia to play for Hakoah. He finally won the representative honours his play had deserved when he captained the Australian national team.

On his return to England he made 34 league appearances for Luton Town before joining Stockport County. He was an ever-present as County won the Fourth Division Championship, but sadly a knee injury ended his career at the age of 37. Woods then had a spell managing Altrincham before returning to Edgeley Park as coach. Six months later he found himself in charge but midway through the 1971-72 season, he was sacked after County had been knocked out of the FA Cup by Blyth Spartans.

HARRY LEYLAND

Goalkeeper Harry Leyland began his Football League career with Everton, but in five seasons at Goodison Park he had made only 36 appearances when he was released in the summer of 1956. Unable to find a new league club, he was on his way to join non-League Tonbridge with team-mate Ron Saunders when Blackburn manager Johnny Carey swooped to sign him as a replacement for Reg Elvy.

A brave and agile 'keeper, he made his Rovers' debut in a 3-1 win at West Ham United in the second game of the 1956-57 season, going on to appear in 106 consecutive League and Cup games from his debut. He was ever-present when the club won promotion to the First Division in 1957-58 and won an FA Cup runners-up medal in 1960.

It was around this time that the Rovers' 'keeper began to suffer from a succession of injuries and midway through the 1960-61 season, Leyland, who had appeared in 188 League and Cup games for the Ewood Park club, was transferred to Tranmere Rovers.

Over the next five seasons with the Wirral-based club, he missed very few games and was ever-present in seasons 1964-65 and 1965-66. The club finished fifth in Division Four in each of these seasons, just missing out on a promotion place.

He went on to play in 194 League and Cup games for the Prenton Park club before bowing out of league football to join Wigan Athletic, where he became player-manager.

MacLeod opted to return to his native Scotland to play for Hibernian. Manager Jack Marshall brought internationals Joe Haverty from Arsenal and Ian Lawther from Sunderland to Ewood Park whilst also securing the services of Preston North End's unsettled goalkeeper Fred Else.

Rovers' new-look side didn't make the best of starts to the 1961-62 season, a goalless draw at home to Cardiff City on the opening day of the campaign was followed by defeats at Blackpool and Manchester United, the latter by 6-1. Unfortunately, Lawther and Haverty were struggling to find form and within a few matches bot were languishing in the reserves.

MICK McGRATH

Mick McGrath joined Rovers from Home Farm in August 1954, but despite some impressive performances in the club's Central League side, he had to wait until April 1956 before making his league debut in a 1-1 draw at Nottingham Forest. In fact, it wasn't until 1957-58, the club's promotion-winning season, when he played in every game, that he established himself fully in the Rovers' side.

This quiet Irishman, along with Ronnie Clayton and Matt Woods, helped form one of the most formidable half-back lines in the club's history.

A hard-tackling wing-half who appeared for the Football League, McGrath was also a regular in the Republic of Ireland side, making 18 full appearances for his country whilst with Rovers.

McGrath also appeared for Rovers in the 1960 FA Cup Final against Wolverhampton Wanderers at Wembley, where he had the misfortune to put through his own goal to open the scoring for the Molineux club. A perfect clubman, Mick McGrath retained his place in the Rovers' side under Jack Marshall until March 1966 when, after scoring 12 goals in 312 League and Cup games, he moved to play for Bradford Park Avenue.

He had the distinction of being the last Bradford player to win an international cap, and not surprisingly was made captain of the Yorkshire club. After making 50 league appearances for Park Avenue he left to play non-League football for Bangor City in the Northern Premier League.

In later years, he returned to Ewood Park to help out with Rovers' youth teams before becoming involved in local junior soccer.

FRED ELSE

Fred Else began his Football League career with Preston North End after impressing for Axwell Park Colliery Welfare FC whilst doing his National Service. He made his league debut for the Lilywhites in a 4-0 win against Manchester City at Deepdale in March 1954 following an injury to George Thompson. By 1956-57, Else was North End's first-choice 'keeper and in his first full season was ever-present as the Deepdale club finished third in Division One. In fact, he impressed so much that he played for England 'B' and was unlucky not to win full international honours.

A firm favourite with the North End fans he was sold to Blackburn Rovers for £17,000 on 11 August 1961 after failing to agree terms. That very same evening, he played for Rovers against North End in a pre-season friendly!

He kept a clean sheet on his Rovers' debut as they drew 0-0 at home to Cardiff City on the opening day of the 1961-62 season. Else was the club's first-choice 'keeper for five seasons, being ever-present in 1963-64 when Rovers finished seventh in the First Division. A broken collar bone in the match against Burnley in February 1965 kept him out of the side for seven games but when he returned to first team action he seemed to have lost a little of his sharpness that had made him one of the top goalkeepers in the country.

Following the club's relegation in 1965-66, Else, who had appeared in 221 League and Cup games for Rovers, left Ewood Park to join Barrow. He made 148 league appearances for the Holker Street club before being appointed their manager for a short spell before their demise from the Football League.

Marshall was forced to play another youngster up front after just a handful of Central League games - his name, John Byrom, and on his seventh appearance he notched a hat-trick in a 3-2 win at West Ham United. Though the club were struggling in the First Division, Rovers' performances in the League Cup were highly entertaining. After winning 3-1 at Peterborough United in the first round, Blackburn were held to a 1-1 draw at Bristol Rovers in round two before Eddie Thomas netted all four goals in the 4-0 replay win at Ewood Park. Rovers followed this up with wins over Nottingham Forest (Away 2-1), Ipswich Town (Home 4-1) and Rotherham United (Away 1-0) to reach the semi-final stage of the competition. Their opponents in the two-legged tie were Fourth Division Rochdale but in the first leg at Spotland, Rovers gave a very poor performance and lost 3-1. A crowd of just 11,644 turned up at Ewood Park for the second leg but Rovers, who were without Else, Woods, Clayton and Lawther, couldn't pull back the first-leg deficit and, though they won 2-1 on the night, went out of the competition 4-3 on aggregate!

Rovers also embarked on a good run in the FA Cup, beating Brighton and Hove Albion (Away 3-0), Stoke City (Away 1-0) and Middlesbrough (Home 2-1) to reach the quarter-finals where their opponents were Fulham. After a 2-2 draw at Craven Cottage, hopes were high of a semi-final place but playing in an unfamiliar all-red strip in the Ewood Park replay, Rovers lost 1-0.

In spite of the club's performances in the two cup competitions, their league form was poor and after losing their last five games of the season, Rovers slumped to 16th place.

Towards the end of that season, Rovers signed inside-forward Bobby Craig from Sheffield Wednesday and he made his mark in the opening game of the 1962-63 season, netting a hat-trick in a 3-3 draw at Ipswich Town. Yet two days later, the same side lost 5-2 at home to Nottingham Forest. Throughout the season, Rovers were involved in a number of high-scoring games, including a 5-5 home draw against Arsenal. The following week Rovers won 5-2 at West Bromwich Albion with Fred Pickering scoring a hat-trick. Pickering was the club's leading scorer with 23 goals in 36 league games, including another hat-trick in a 5-1 defeat of Wolverhampton Wanderers. That win was one of five successive victories at the end of the season, the best of which was a 6-1 trouncing of Birmingham City, as

Rovers finished the campaign in 11th place.

After losing the opening game of the 1963-64 season, 2-1 at home to Liverpool, Rovers gained two away wins at Sheffield United (1-0) and Aston Villa (2-1) before drawing 2-2 in the return match against the Blades. On 7 September 1963, Rovers entertained Tottenham Hotspur and in one of the greatest displays of attacking football ever seen at Ewood Park, beat the White Hart Lane club 7-2. Bryan Douglas was in irrepressible form and it was he who opened the scoring after quarter-of-an-hour. Andy McEvoy netted twice to give the Rovers a 3-0 lead but goals from Jimmy Greaves and Dave Mackay just before half-time suggested that the second period would be a closely fought affair. However, Andy McEvoy netted another brace to take his total to four goals and, with Mike England and Fred Pickering also finding the net, Rovers completely overwhelmed their illustrious opponents.

McEvoy and Pickering began to establish themselves as the club's main strike force. A Fred Pickering hat-trick helped Rovers beat Everton 4-2 at Goodison Park whilst Andy McEvoy grabbed a hat-trick in a 3-1 win at West Bromwich Albion. A week later, Pickering netted another treble in a 4-1 home win over Arsenal. On Boxing Day 1963, Rovers travelled to Upton Park to face West Ham United and with McEvoy and Pickering both scoring hat-tricks, beat the Hammers 8-2. The win took Rovers to the top of the First Division but two days later they lost 3-1 at home to West Ham!

McEvoy, who netted five hat-Tricks for the club during 1963-64, including one in a 4-0 FA Cup third round win over Grimsby Town, also found the net in round four as Fulham were beaten 2-0. Yet he failed to find the net in the fifth round as Rovers were surprisingly beaten by League newcomers, Fourth Division Oxford United, 3-1.

However, Rovers bounced back with a 5-0 win at Bolton Wanderers and a 5-2 defeat of Leicester City at Filbert Street, a match in which Andy McEvoy scored four of Rovers' goals. Three days after this win, Rovers were rocked by a transfer request by Fred Pickering and he moved to Everton for a club record fee of £80,000. Within a week the two clubs met at Ewood Park but with Everton winning 2-1, Rovers' interest in the League Championship was effectively over. Rovers, in fact, won only one of their last eight games of the season and finished the campaign in seventh place in the First Division.

MIKE ENGLAND

A member of Blackburn Rovers' FA Youth Cup winning side of 1959, Mike England played for the Ewood Park club at outside-right, half-back and centre-forward before settling in central defence where he was acknowledged as arguably the best young centre-half in the country. Though he made his league debut in a 4-1 home defeat at the hands of Preston North End in October 1959, it was 1963-64 before he established himself as the club's first choice centre-half.

He made his debut for Wales against Northern Ireland in April 1962 and by the time of his £95,000 transfer to Tottenham Hotspur in August 1966, England, who had scored 21 goals in 184 League and Cup games for Rovers, had won 20 full caps to go with eleven at Under-23 level. The fee was a Football League record sum for a defender.

England was a key element in the rebuilding of the Tottenham side following the break-up of the legendary double team. His influence was immediate as Spurs won the FA Cup in 1967, the League Cup in 1971, the UEFA Cup in 1972 and the League Cup again in 1973. He went on to win 44 caps for Wales but in March 1975, disheartened by Spurs' abrupt decline, he decided to retire. However, he re-emerged the following August to play 40 games for Cardiff City, helping them to win promotion from Division Three. He then spent four summers playing for Seattle and appeared for Team America in the Bi-centennial Tournament with England, Brazil and Italy in 1976.

He later returned to these shores to become Welsh national team manager and in 1984 he was awarded the MBE for his services to Welsh soccer.

The Blue and Whites

During the summer of 1964, Rovers travelled to the United States to take part in an international tournament but returned home with only one win to show from six matches.

After just two games of the 1964-65 season, manager Jack Marshall reinstated John Byrom into the Rovers' team and his partnership with Andy McEvoy proved a fruitful one. The strikers netted two goals apiece in a 4-1 defeat of Wolverhampton Wanderers whilst McEvoy scored a hat-trick in a 4-0 home win over Sheffield United. When Rovers won 5-2 at Nottingham Forest, McEvoy netted another hat-trick with Byrom scoring twice, and then in the 5-1 defeat of Aston Villa the roles were reversed with

ANDY McEVOY

Originally an inside-forward, Andy McEvoy had been converted into a wing-half and spent most of his early career at Ewood Park in the club's Central League side. However, Jack Marshall later restored him to his original position and he became the Football League's leading scorer.

McEvoy joined Rovers from Bray Wanderers in October 1956 but had to wait until April 1959 before making his league debut, when he scored twice in a 3-1 home win over Luton Town.

Towards the end of the 1962-63 season, Marshall partnered McEvoy with Pickering and though the move wasn't an instant success, he persevered and in 1963-64 it paid dividends. McEvoy scored 32 goals in 37 games, including four in each of the wins over Tottenham Hotspur (Home 7-2) and Leicester City (Away 5-2) and a hat-trick against West Ham United (Away 8-2). McEvoy topped the scoring charts again in 1964-65, his total of 29 goals, including further hat-tricks in the defeats of Sheffield United (Home 4-0) and Nottingham Forest (Away 5-2), saw him finish the First Division's joint leading goalscorer with Jimmy Greaves.

In 1965-66, McEvoy netted his sixth and final hat-trick for the club in a 4-1 FA Cup win over West Ham United. Following the club's relegation to the Second Division, McEvoy, who was a regular in the Republic of Ireland side, spent most of his time back in the club's reserve team and, after scoring 103 goals in 213 League and Cup games, returned to Ireland where he became a tram driver and played football on a part-time basis for Limerick.

Byrom scoring a hat-trick and McEvoy a brace. Byrom netted another treble in a 4-0 home win over West Ham United to finish the season with 25 goals. McEvoy's haul of 29 was enough for him to finish joint top-scorer in the First Division with Spurs' Jimmy Greaves. The penultimate game of the season, in which Rovers finished tenth, saw the club play out another 5-5 draw at Birmingham City!

The low point of the campaign was without doubt the third round of the League Cup when, after drawing 0-0 at Third Division Workington, Rovers crashed out of the competition with a 5-1 defeat at home to the Cumbrian outfit!

An outbreak of polio in the town led to the cancellation of the opening fixtures of the 1965-66 season. When Rovers' season did get underway, they were without former England international Bryan Douglas and only managed one win from their opening eight games, the other seven matches all being lost. The club's only success was a 3-2 home win over Fulham - the only match that season in which both Byrom and McEvoy scored! Following Douglas's return, Rovers won one and drew two of the next three matches, including a 4-1 win at Burnley. With Byrom and McEvoy finding goals hard to come by, manager Jack Marshall moved Mike England to centre-forward and recalled George Jones in a new striking partnership. Though results still continued to go against them, Rovers managed a couple of big wins against Nottingham Forest (Home 5-0) and Northampton Town (Home 6-1) with Jones netting a hat-trick in this latter match. Jones, in fact, scored nine goals in nine games before injury forced him out of the side.

Despite the threat of relegation hanging over the club, Rovers embarked on an FA Cup run which took them to the quarter-finals, a run in which both Byrom and McEvoy inexplicably found their scoring boots! After a 3-0 home win over Arsenal in round three, a John Byrom hat-trick gave Rovers a 3-3 draw at West Ham United, quickly followed by an Andy McEvoy treble in the replay which Rovers won 4-1. Rovers needed two games to beat Norwich City but then went out of the competition at the hands of Sheffield Wednesday. By the time they made their exit, Rovers were as good as relegated. In the second half of the season, Rovers won three and lost 18 of their matches with the result that they finished bottom of the First Division with just 20 points!

FRED PICKERING

When he turned professional with Blackburn Rovers in 1958, Fred Pickering was being groomed as a full-back but with the club so well served in that department, his opportunities were limited. He had enjoyed success in the Rovers' junior teams, helping to win the FA Youth Cup in 1959, but when given a first team chance he had failed to make a lasting impression. After some powerful displays at centre-forward in the reserves, he was given a chance in that position in the first team and soon went on to make quite a name for himself. In 1962-63 he scored 23 goals in 36 games, including hat-tricks against West Bromwich Albion (Away 5-2) and Wolverhampton Wandereers (Home 5-1). His total of 23 goals in 1963-64 included further trebles in the wins over Everton (Away 4-2) and West Ham United (Away 8-2). He later became unsettled and wanted a transfer, the Rovers' board allowing him to join Everton for £85,000.

He began well by scoring a hat-trick on his home debut against Nottingham Forest and became one of only four players this century who have achieved hat-tricks when making their debuts for England - this he did against the USA in May 1964. After scoring 27 goals in 1964-65, injuries hampered his Goodison career and in August 1967 he moved to Birmingham City for £50,000. He returned to Lancashire in 1969 when Blackpool paid £45,000 to secure his services. After helping the Seasiders win promotion to the First Division, he rejoined Blackburn in March 1971.

Pickering was cast in the role of saviour as Rovers faced Third Division football for the first time in their history. He had taken his tally of goals to 74 in 158 games when manager Ken Furphy decided he was out of condition and let him go to Brighton and Hove Albion, where he ended his league career.

Though Marshall's contract was not renewed, he was retained on a weekly contract and immediately set about rebuilding the team. Having failed to entice Huddersfield Town to part with Alan Gilliver prior to the previous season's transfer deadline day, he returned to Leeds Road to sign the bustling centre-forward. He also bought Preston North End's reserve goalkeeper John Barton to replace Fred Else, and Welsh international wing-half Barrie Hole from Cardiff City for £40,000. On the eve of the 1966-

67 season, Rovers received £95,000 when Mike England moved to Tottenham Hotspur.

The new season got off to a good start when Rovers won 3-2 at Derby County on the opening day of the campaign. This was followed by home wins over Charlton Athletic and Crystal Palace, both by a 2-1 score-line. In September 1966, Marshall pulled off a major coup by signing Manchester United's World Cup winger John Connellly. Despite all the new signings, Rovers failed to find any level of consistency and so approached former Blackburn favourite Eddie Quigley to join the club as coach. Quigley, who was manager at Stockport County, insisted on being given the title of assistant-manager and sole responsibility for coaching throughout the club. His arrival coincided with the news that the Football League commission had found in their favour with regard to the injury problems that Gilliver had suffered since his move from Huddersfield and that the Yorkshire club should repay some of the £18,000 that Rovers had paid for his services.

Following a shock FA Cup exit at the hands of Carlisle United, the club parted company with Jack Marshall, who, unhappy with a number of aspects of life at Ewood Park, tendered his resignation. Eddie Quigley became caretaker-manager and in his first match in charge led Rovers to a 1-0 win over Bristol City, courtesy of a John Connelly goal. The win over the Robins was the start of a five-match winning sequence which put the Rovers back into the promotion-chasing pack. The crunch came on Easter Saturday but a 1-0 defeat at home to Coventry City condemned the club to another season of Second Division football.

Hopes of promotion were high when Rovers won the first three games of the 1967-68 season and, in fact, the club lost only one of the campaign's opening nine fixtures. After three successive defeats, Rovers bounced back with a 5-3 win at Preston North End but in the second half of the season, Rovers' promotion ambitions fell away and only a four-match winning run in March lifted the gloom that had fallen on Ewood Park. Towards the end of the campaign, attendances began to plummet as Rovers failed to win any of their last seven games, ending the season in eighth place.

During the summer of 1968, Mike Ferguson was sold to Aston Villa for £50,000 and within a few weeks, he was joined at Villa Park by Barrie

MIKE FERGUSON

Mike Ferguson was playing as an inside-forward for Accrington Stanley when, following their resignation from the Football League in 1961, he became a target for both Blackburn Rovers and Preston North End. In the end, Rovers' manager Jack Marshall paid £1,500 for his services and under his guidance, Ferguson was converted into an outside-right.

He was a natural crowd pleaser, revelling in the style of football that Rovers played under Marshall. Not content on beating an opponent, he would wait for him to recover and then go back and beat him again! Despite being the scorer of some memorable goals, Ferguson had a suspect temperament, which came to a head in the match against Coventry City on Easter Saturday 1967. He was sent-off after lashing out at a Sky Blues' defender following a stiff challenge. The game was a vital promotion clash and after Rovers had lost 1-0, they had to be content with fourth place in Division Two, whilst Coventry went on to win promotion to the top flight.

Ferguson stayed at Ewood Park for another season, but in May 1968, after scoring 36 goals in 248 League and Cup games, he was sold to Aston Villa for £50,000. After just one season at Villa Park, he

moved to Queen's Park Rangers where the London club's style of play suited him. He later played for Cambridge United and Rochdale before trying his luck in Iceland with IA Akranes.

On his return to England he played in a couple of games for Halifax Town before embarking on a career in coaching which took him to all parts of the world. After a brief spell managing Enfield, he took charge of Evagoras in Cyprus but has now moved back to live in his home-town of Burnley.

KEITH NEWTON

Keith Newton arrived at Ewood Park as a gangling inside-forward having been spotted playing for Spurley Hey youth club in the Manchester junior leagues. He was a member of Rovers' FA Youth Cup winning side of 1959, having appeared at centre-half before being switched to left-back.

A cultured defender, he was sharp in the tackle and sound in the air. He was also noted for his attacking runs down the flank. He finally settled into the right-back spot and won his first major honour in 1964, when he gained the first of four Under-23 caps against Scotland at Newcastle.

Shortly after this he suffered the first of several major injuries which dogged his career and cost him many representative honours. He won his first full cap in February 1965 against West Germany at Wembley but it ended in near disaster. He was carried off the field with a suspected broken leg just before the interval, but the injury turned out to be less serious than feared. These injuries hampered his early career and he just missed out on inclusion in the 1966 World Cup.

Newton, who was rated a world-class player, had scored 10 goals in 357 League and Cup games for Rovers when in December 1969 he was transferred to Everton for £80,000.

He helped the Goodison club win the 1969-70 League Championship, but after this success became more and more unsettled at the way he was being asked to play and finally lost his place. In June 1972 he moved to Burnley on a free transfer, helping the Clarets to win promotion to the First Division in 1972-73. He remained at Turf Moor for the rest of his career, playing in 252 gmes before finally bowing out at the end of the 1977-78 season. He later had brief spells with Morecambe and Clitheroe. Sadly, he passed away in the summer of 1998.

Hole, whose transfer netted £60,000 for the Ewood Park club.

Once again, Rovers began the season in fine style, winning three and drawing two of the opening five games. Despite losing their next two games, they were the only defeats in the first 13 games of the campaign, placing Rovers in the promotion pack. It was during this period that Don Martin scored one of the most controversial goals in the club's history against Sheffield United. The former Northampton striker bundled former England 'keeper Alan Hodgkinson and the ball over the line to give Rovers a 1-0 win. However, goals were still hard to come by and in October 1968, Rovers signed Jim Fryatt, the Stockport County centre-forward, for £25,000 and though he didn't score, he had an immediate effect, making two of the goals in a 3-1 win at Bury. Fryatt scored twice in a 3-2 win over Birmingham City, for whom former Rovers' favourite Fred Pickering scored both their goals. However, after this win, results fell away and it was only in the FA Cup that Rovers' fans had something to cheer. After beating Stockport County (Home 2-0) and Portsmouth (Home 4-0), in which Malcolm Darling netted a hat-trick, Rovers were drawn at home to Manchester City in round five. A crowd of 42,315 gathered to witness a disappointing display by Blackburn, who were beaten 4-1.

Rovers won just one of their last 16 games of the 1968-69 season, a sequence which ended with the club in 19th position in Division Two, the lowest finishing position in the club's history at that time.

Though a familiar face in Johnny Carey returned to the club in the newly created position of administrative manager, the 1968-9 season also saw the end of Ronnie Clayton and Bryan Douglas's first-class careers as they both announced their retirement from the game.

During the close season, Quigley began to prepare for a major rebuilding programme by releasing seven of his first team squad and signing three new players. These were Brian Hill from Huddersfield Town, Allan Hunter from Oldham Athletic and Ken Knighton from Preston North End. Adopting a new 4-3-3 formation, Rovers made a good start to the 1969-70 season, winning three and drawing two of their opening five matches. In fact, they only lost two of their first 13 fixtures and by Christmas were top of the Second Division. Middlesbrough and Millwall had both been beaten 4-0, with Don Martin netting a hat-trick against the Lions, and Preston North End 4-2, with John Connelly also scoring a hat-trick. Yet despite these successes, there had been a couple of defeats - 3-0 at Birmingham City and 4-0 at Sheffield United - that proved Rovers' defence could be exploited.

Just before Christmas, Keith Newton was sold to Everton for a fee of £80,000 but the Rovers' chairman said that the money would be used to reduce the club's outstanding debts rather than for strengthening the team. For the game at Hull City on Boxing Day, Rovers' manager Eddie Quigley had planned to play Eamon Rogers at right-back but he refused and Frank Kopel, who had been on the transfer list for two months, took his place.

DON MARTIN

A former England Youth international, Don Martin was a member of the Northampton Town side which won promotion to the First Division in 1964-65, but after scoring 53 goals in 136 league games, he left the Cobblers to join Blackburn Rovers in February 1968 for a fee of £30,000.

Martin made his Rovers' debut in a goalless draw at home to Norwich City and, though he had been a proven goalscorer at the County Ground, his perceptive use of the ball and reading of the game meant that he could also be used in midfield. After topping the club's scoring charts in 1969-70 with 13 goals, including a hat-trick in a 4-0 home win over Millwall, Martin broke his ankle early the following season, an injury which threatened to end his career. By the time he had regained full fitness, Rovers had a new manager and were in the Third Division. Under Ken Furphy, Martin found himself playing most of his football in the club's Central League side, but when Gordon Lee replaced Furphy following his departure to Sheffield United, Martin's career was resurrected.

His career enjoyed an 'Indian summer' and in 1974-75 when Rovers won the Third Division Championship. He topped the club's goalscoring charts again, his total of 15 goals including another hat-trick in the 4-1 defeat of Gillingham. He had scored 64 goals in 251 League and Cup games for Rovers when in November 1975 he was allowed to rejoin his first club to finish his League career.

During his two spells with Northampton, Martin scored 82 goals in 252 games before deciding to retire.

Rovers lost 3-0 and then the following day went down by the same score-line at home to Portsmouth, a match in which Rogers condescended to play at right-back! There then followed an embarrassing defeat at the hands of Swindon Town in the third round of the FA Cup before Rovers lost 4-1 at Middlesbrough in the league. The club's promotion hopes were now fading with the lack of goals being the major problem.

With the supporters expecting Rovers to strengthen the attack, manager Quigley invested £30,000 in Bournemouth's England Under-23 goal-keeper Roger Jones but in only his fourth appearance for the club - a 1-1 draw at home to Birmingham City - he strained his groin on an icy Ewood pitch and didn't play again until the final game of the season. Their opponents in this game were Swindon Town, who Rovers had beaten 2-0 on the opening day of the season but who completely outplayed the Ewood Park club in the FA Cup. The Robins won 1-0 leaving Rovers in eighth place in Division Two.

Towards the end of the season, the club had parted company with John Coddington and Jim Fryatt and in the close season gave free transfers to two more experienced campaigners in internationals Adam Blacklaw and John Connelly. To strengthen the squad, Quigley paid out a club record fee of £60,000 to bring Bury's young midfield star Jimmy Kerr to Ewood Park.

Injury kept Kerr out of the side for the club's first five games of the 1970-71 season, only one of which was won. Even when he did return to duty, he had to wait until his ninth appearance before the club won a game, beating Norwich City 2-1. Sadly, in his eleventh game he received an injury which ended his playing career. This came on top of Don Martin's broken ankle, which he suffered in a 1-1 draw at Sheffield Wednesday in the third game of the season. The club won just one of its first 13 matches and, after a first round exit in the League Cup at Bolton Wanderers, the directors tried to turn things around by asking Johnny Carey and Eddie Quigley to swap duties!

Midway through the season, the club had won only three league games and relegation to the Third Division looked a distinct possibility. With the club also struggling financially, Carey had no alternative but to sell Ken Knighton to Hull City. The directors made a small amount of cash available to Carey and in March 1971, Fred Pickering rejoined the Rovers from Blackpool, whom he had helped win promotion to the First Division.

Though he was cast in the role of a Messiah, Pickering was overweight and troubled by injury and was most certainly not the player that had left Ewood Park seven years earlier. On 27 April 1971, Rovers visited Queen's Park Rangers where a 2-0 defeat consigned them to the Third Division for the first time in their history.

In June 1971 Rovers announced that they were to part company with both Carey and Quigley as preparations were made for the club's first season of Third Division football.

Rovers' new boss was Ken Furphy, the manager of Watford, whom he had taken to an FA Cup semi-final. Goals from Rogers and 18-year-old Gerry McDonald, who was making his league debut, gave Rovers a 2-1 win over Rotherham United on the opening day of the 1971-72 season. However, the club soon hit a slump, losing three games in succession - Bournemouth (Away 0-1) Chesterfield (Away 0-2) and Bolton Wanderers (Home 0-3) - whilst in early October, Rovers were beaten 7-1 by Shrewsbury Town!

With little money to spend on strengthening the squad, Furphy needed to sell before he could make the changes that were so obviously necessary. Northern Ireland international centre-half Allan Hunter was sold to Ipswich Town for £60,000. Furphy returned to Vicarage Road to sign midfielder Terry Garbett and then to Newcastle United for the Magpies' Danish international Ben Arentoft. Later in the season he snapped up Tony Field from Southport for £17,500 plus Freddie Goodwin. He also bought another striker to the club when he signed Barry Endean from Charlton Athletic. Despite these new acquisitions, by the end of November, Rovers had been knocked out of both cup competitions and were next-to-bottom of the Third Division!

It was then that Ken Furphy made probably his most important signing when he brought Newcastle United centre-half John McNamee to Ewood Park. With Derek Fazackerley being reinstated into the team alongside him, the two formed the best central defensive partnership in the Third Division. After a 3-1 win at Tranmere Rovers on his debut, McNamee was only on the losing side once in his first nine games. Tony Field found his shooting boots and was the club's leading scorer by far with 17 goals in 33 games, including a hat-trick in a 4-0 home win over Barnsley. The improvement in results meant that Rovers ended the season in tenth

STUART METCALFE

A former Blackburn Schoolboys player who went on to represent England at youth level, Stuart Metcalfe joined his home-town club in March 1964. He was a member of the club's Central League Championship-winning side of 1966-67 and the following season made his Football League debut in a 1-1 home draw against Cardiff City.

By the time he had turned 18, Metcalfe had established himself as a first team regular in the Rovers' side, and though most of his early games were at outside-right, it wasn't long before Eddie Quigley moved him into a more central midfield position.

After the club were relegated to the Third Division in 1970-71, Metcalfe experienced some difficulties in the more physical approach to the game in the lower divisions. Eventually, under Ken Furphy and more so under Gordon Lee, Metcalfe began to blossom. His probing passes and strong running complemented the hard-working Tony Parkes to give Rovers one of the strongest midfield departments in the Third Division. When Rovers won the Third Division title in 1974-75, Metcalfe, who wasn't a prolific scorer, had his best season, netting seven in 43 appearances.

He was awarded a testimonial in 1978, but when the club won promotion to the Second Division again in 1979-80 following their relegation the previous season, Metcalfe was no longer a regular member of the Rovers' side. He left Ewood Park in July 1980 to join Carlisle United.

He spent two seasons at Brunton Park before having a short spell in the United States with Carolina Lightning. In October 1982 he rejoined Blackburn Rovers as a non-contract player and took his total of League and Cup appearances, in which he scored 25 goals, to 434 before ending his Football League career with Crewe Alexandra.

ROGER JONES

Roger Jones might well have slipped out of League football when Portsmouth decided to scrap their reserve team in the late 1960s, but fortunately south coast neighbours Bournemouth recognised his potential and took him to Dean Court. Whilst with the Cherries, Jones developed into one of the best goalkeepers outside the First Division and had won England Under-23 honours when Blackburn manager Eddie Quigley paid £30,000 for his services in January 1970.

Although injury restricted his appearances in the first few months after he had joined Rovers, Jones went on to prove himself one of the club's best-ever 'keepers.

Although not the tallest of men, Jones totally dominated his six-yard box where his judges of crosses was superb. Had he been playing in a higher class of football, there is no doubt that Jones' world-class saves would have brought him international recognition. He went on to break the club's record for goalkeeping appearances, later beaten by Terry Gennoe.

Jones, who kept 16 clean sheets during Rovers' Third Division Championship winning season of 1974-75, had appeared in 272 League and Cup games when he was allowed to join Newcastle United in March 1976 for a ridiculously low fee of £20,000. Because of Jones' history of knee trouble, it was agreed that the sum would be paid in instalments depending on the number of games he played. Jones only appeared in five games for the Magpies so they refused to pay the fee.

The next stop in Jones' career took him to Stoke City, where he made 101 League appearances before joining Derby County in the summer of 1980. He appeared in 59 games for the Rams and had a brief loan spell with Birmingham City before joining York City. He played in 122 games for the Minstermen, helping them win the Fourth Division Championship in 1983-84.

After a spell coaching with the Bootham Crescent club, he moved to Sunderland in a similar capacity before acting as assistant-manager to Malcolm Crosby when the Wearsiders reached the FA Cup Final in 1992.

position.

Even before the 1972-73 season started, the club were hampered by a number of injuries and suspensions and so began the campaign with many first teamers on the side-lines. By the middle of October, Rovers had won just three of their opening 14 games and had occupied last place in the Third Division on three separate occasions!

On 21 October 1972, Rovers travelled to Swansea City and drew 2-2, the first match in a run of 19 consecutive league games without defeat. The Ewood Park club won 12 and drew seven of those matches, rising from next to bottom of the Third Division to fifth place. However, the team then lost two games in the space of four days, the latter of these at home to Chesterfield. The Spireites had been Rovers' opponents on Boxing Day and had left Ewood Park with a 1-0 win. However, Rovers' unbeaten record remained intact when it was discovered that Chesterfield's goalkeeper Jim Brown had not been eligible to play because his registration forms had been delayed in the post. The Football League then decided that the match should be replayed but despite Rovers being on the fringe of the promotion pack, lowly Chesterfield again won 1-0. Following Rovers' 1-0 win at Bolton Wanderers on 28 March 1973, when Derek Fazcakerley scored with a powerful header, the Ewood Park club were in equal second place with Notts County and Oldham Athletic. All three teams had 46 points but Rovers had to play both of their promotion rivals before the end of the season.

On Easter Saturday, Rovers travelled to Meadow Lane to take on Notts County, who, though on equal points, had a superior goal average to Rovers. With Roger Jones in outstanding form, Rovers came away with a point in a goalless draw, but then a disappointing 1-1 draw at already relegated Scunthorpe United left Rovers needing a win against Oldham Athletic on the final day of the season and hope that Notts County lost against Tranmere Rovers. Unfortunately Rovers could only draw against the Latics whilst Notts County beat Tranmere to join champions Bolton Wanderers in the Second Division.

Rovers made an indifferent start to the 1973-74 season, winning three and losing six of their first nine games, but after beating Brighton and Hove Albion 3-1 on 6 October 1973, embarked on a run of ten unbeaten league games that saw them move up the table at a rapid rate. The final game of this sequence saw them beat Watford 5-0, it was Rovers' finest performance of the season. A week later, Rovers played out a goalless draw at non-League Willington in the FA Cup before winning the replay 6-1. They accounted for another non-League club in Altrincham in round two before crashing out of the competition to Everton, who beat Rovers 3-0 at Goodison Park. However, just when it looked as if the club were mounting a serious promotion challenge, manager Ken Furphy was lured to take charge of First Division Sheffield United. Richard Dinnis became the club's caretaker-manager until Gordon Lee was appointed in January 1974. The new manager was handicapped by injuries and suspensions when he arrived at Ewood Park, so it was all the more surprising that he allowed Terry Garbett and leading scorer Tony Field to join Furphy at Bramall Lane. On 27 January 1974 the club had its first experience of Sunday football when Ewood's biggest crowd of the season, 10,989, turned up to watch Rovers beat Shrewsbury Town 2-0. Towards the end of the season, a run of six undefeated league games, including five draws in succession, helped Rovers to a mid-table placing of 13th.

During the close season, Lee made a umber of important signings. His first capture was winger Pat Hilton from Brighton and Hove Albion on a free transfer, quickly followed by his Seagulls' team-mate Ken Beamish, who cost the club £25,000. He then snapped up Preston North End's experienced central defender Graham Hawkins and Bradford City's utility player Graham Oates before early in the season adding Rotherham United's Jimmy Mullen and Halifax Town's Andy Burgin to his squad.

At start of the 1974-75 season, Rover lost just one of their opening 12 games - the highlight being the 4-1 home win over Gillingham in which long-serving Don Martin netted a hat-trick. Manager Gordon Lee had restored Martin to the side to partner the direct-running of Ken Beamish and it certainly seemed to be paying dividends as Rovers, despite a 6-3 reversal at Hereford United, topped the Third Division at the turn of the year. However, a 1-0 home defeat by Peterborough United, in which Jimmy Mullen broke a leg, was quickly followed by a crucial defeat at fellow promotion candidates Plymouth Argyle. The 2-1 defeat at Home Park saw the Devon club leap-frog over them to take over the top spot. Lee replaced the injured Mullen with Grimsby Town's Mike Hickman, who cost the club £10,000, and he helped Rovers win their next match, scoring the opening

DEREK FAZACKERLEY

Derek Fazackerley's breakthrough into the Blackburn Rovers first team - he made his league debut in a goalless draw at Hull City in February 1971 - coincided with one of the bleakest periods in the club's history. But through it all 'Faz', as he was fondly known to all Rovers' supporters, remained unperturbed at the heart of the defence, turning in his usually reliable performances week after week.

Dominant in the air and a strong tackler, he was the cornerstone of the Blackburn defence with his greatest asset being his consistency. It was a tribute to his performances that on the rare occasions he had a bad match, it was noticed immediately as being totally out of character. He was extremely quick over the ground, his pace enabling him to recover lost ground with ease. He was always at his best when playing alongside a traditional centre-half, almost as a sweeper.

Although he didn't score too many goals for Rovers - 25 in all - one of his more important came when he scored the only goal of a tension-charged local derby against Bolton Wanderers at Burnden Park in March 1973.

Derek Fazackerley was 'Mr Consistency' to the majority of Ewood supporters and when he passed Ronnie Clayton's all-time appearance record for Blackburn Rovers, he wrote a new page in the history of the club. Fazackerley had played in 674 League and Cup games when in 1987 he was allowed to join Chester City as player assistant-manager. A year later he joined former Rovers' boss Bob Saxton at York City before, in February 1989, he teamed up with his old friend Martin Dobson at Bury.

In May 1990 he was appointed player-manager of the Finnish club Kumu before returning to the League scene as reserve team coach at Newcastle. Appointed first team coach at St James Park in 1992, he played an important part in helping the Magpies win the First Division title in 1992-93. Since then, Fazackerley has helped Kevin Keegan with the England set-up.

goal in a 2-1 defeat of Bury. A week later, Rovers entertained Plymouth Argyle in a top of the table clash. A crowd of 17,818 saw Argyle race into a 2-0 lead but as half-time approached, Ken Beamish reduced the arrears with a close-range header. The second-half was all one-way traffic as Rovers dominated the proceedings. Martin levelled the scores and two minutes later, Hickman gave Rovers the lead. Further goals by Hickman and Martin saw Rovers run out winners 5-2 and restore the Ewood Park club to the top of the table, though they couldn't pull away from Argyle owing to the fact that too many of their games had been drawn. Promotion was finally achieved on 19 April 1975 when goals from Metcalfe and Hickman helped defeat Chesterfield 2-0. Plymouth had booked their spot in the Second Division a few days earlier! A 2-0 defeat at Colchester United three days later meant that the title would not be settled until the final days of the campaign. A magnificent 4-1 win at Port Vale, coupled with Argyle's surprise defeat at Peterborough United, meant that the Third Division title was as good as being Blackburn's. The club's final game of the season at home to Wrexham was watched by an Ewood Park crowd of 21,290, who saw Rovers play out a goalless draw and thus lift the Third Division Championship.

The final placings were as follows:

	P.	W.	D.	L.	F.	A.	Pts
Blackburn Rovers	46	22	16	8	68	45	60
Plymouth Argyle	46	24	11	11	79	58	59
Charlton Athletic	46	22	11	13	76	61	55

The joy of winning promotion to the Second Division was soon shattered when it was announced that Gordon Lee was to leave Ewood Park and take charge at managerless Newcastle United. The managerial position was filled when the Rovers' board persuaded Jim Smith to leave Colchester United.

The pre-season began well with Rovers qualifying for the knockout stages of the Anglo-Scottish Cup, and this form was carried over into the League with the club taking five points from their opening three games including a 4-1 win over Oldham Athletic. However, four successive league defeats followed and with the club being knocked out of the League Cup by Preston North End and the Anglo-Scottish Cup by Motherwell, the manager began to search for new blood. He returned to his former club to sign striker Bobby Svarc for £25,000, although his arrival didn't signal an immediate change in Rovers' fortunes.

On 8 November 1975, the club celebrated its centenary when neighbours Bolton Wanderers visited Ewood Park for a Second Division fixture. A crowd of 24,430, the largest attendance for a league match since March 1967, saw the sides play out a 1-1 draw with Graham Oates scoring for Rovers. Full-backs Heaton and Burgin both picked up injuries which ultimately ended their careers, whilst latest signing Bobby Svarc was forced to undergo a cartilage operation. As the transfer deadline day approached, Gordon Lee returned to Ewood Park to sign Roger Jones and Graham Oates, whilst Jim Smith paid around £20,000 to bring Wolves' winger David Wagstaffe and former Bolton wide man Gordon Taylor, then with Birmingham City, to Ewood Park. Their experience helped the club win five of their next six games, including wins over Easter against Carlisle United (Home 1-0) and York City (Home 4-0), thus ensuring the club's Second Division survival with a finishing position of 15th.

After a 3-1 win over Bolton Wanderers on the opening day of the 1976-77 season, Rovers lost four successive league games and made a second round exit in the League Cup at the hands of Stockport County. Within the first few weeks of the campaign, Smith had made two important signings in Glenn Keeley, a young centre-half from Newcastle United, and former Blackburn favourite John Byrom who rejoined the club from Bolton Wanderers.

On 2 October 1976, Blackburn Rovers became the first club to have a red card shown to one of its players during a league match. Following the introduction of the red and yellow card system, David Wagstaffe received his marching orders for dissent in a 1-0 win at Orient. Throughout the months of October and November, Rovers won seven of nine games played, with their best result being a 6-1 defeat of Notts County. The club continued to make a gradual improvement, ending the season in 12th place. During the course of the campaign the FA decided to impose a transfer ban on the club following a dispute with Newcastle United. Rovers had failed to settle payments for the transfer of Glenn Keeley, owing somewhere in the region of £15,000. Problems stemmed back to the controver-

JOHN BYROM

A former England Youth international, John Byrom made his Rovers' debut in a 2-0 home win over Birmingham City in November 1961, but over the next three seasons found himself in and out of the Blackburn side. When Fred Pickering was sold to Everton, Byrom was given an extended run in the Rovers' side and responded with 25 goals in 40 games in 1964-65, including hat-tricks against Aston Villa (Home 5-1) and West Ham United (Home 4-0). However, after both he and Andy McEvoy lost their goalscoring touch, Byrom was allowed to join Bolton Wanderers for £25,000 in the summer of 1966.

Initially he had linked well with Wyn Davies and Francis Lee but within a couple of months both had left Burnden Park. It was 1969-70 before Byrom found his shooting boots. He netted hat-tricks in the first two games of the season and ended the campaign with 25 goals. The following season Bolton were relegated and as the club's most saleable asset he was made available for transfer. Deciding to stay at Burnden Park, Byrom helped the Wanderers win the Third Division Championship in 1972-73 and netted a memorable hat-trick the following season in a 3-2 FA Cup defeat of First Division Stoke City. He had scored 130 goals in 351 games for the Wanderers before being given a free transfer in 1976 and returning to Ewood Park.

Though a series of injuries hampered his return, he took his tally of goals for the Rovers to 64 in 149 League and Cup outings before retiring at the end of the 1976-77 season.

49

sial departure of Gordon Lee the previous summer and the fact that 'keeper Roger Jones had joined the Magpies in a deal which involved payments linked to the number of appearances that he made. Jones made only five appearances for Newcastle and though he had a history of knee trouble, he went on to serve several league clubs after leaving St James Park. Happily, the transfer embargo was short-lived with the Ewood club settling all outstanding payments within a matter of weeks.

Because of the club's financial problems, the only new players to arrive at Ewood during the close season were both free transfers - full-back John Curtis from Blackpool and winger Noel Brotherston from Tottenham Hotspur. Following an indifferent start to the 1977-78 season, Rovers began to pick up points and after a seven-match unbeaten run towards the end of the year gave the supporters hope that the club could mount a serious promotion challenge. One of the teams beaten during that spell was Southampton, one of the promotion favourites, who went down 2-1 after having both Steve Williams and Peter Osgood sent-off! On Boxing Day, Rovers travelled to Turf Moor to take on local rivals Burnley. First-half goals from Wagstaffe, Fear and Brotherston gave Rovers a commanding 3-0 lead at the interval but after Fear, who was on loan from Bristol City, missed a penalty early in the second-half, Rovers found themselves hanging on at the final whistle after the Clarets had pulled two goals back. On the final day of 1977, Rovers lost 4-0 at leaders Tottenham Hotspur and three matches later were beaten 5-2 by Blackpool, results that posed serious questions about the club's chances of winning promotion. Manager Jim Smith paid £35,000 to West Ham United for the services of former Arsenal striker John Radford in a bid to boost the club's promotion push. Though he scored in his first match as Rovers beat Oldham Athletic 4-2, it wasn't long before the club were rocked by the news that Jim Smith had departed to become the manager of Birmingham City. Norman Bodell, Smith's assistant took temporary charge of team affairs but with just four games left, Jim Iley, the manager of Barnsley, accepted the offer to take over the reins at Ewood Park. Though Rovers failed to win any of their remaining games, they ended the campaign in fifth place, their highest position since 1966-67.

Rovers made a disastrous start to the 1978-79 season, winning just one of their opening ten league games - 3-0 over Orient - and losing 2-1 to Third Division Exeter City in the League Cup. Iley moved into the transfer market, paying £40,000 for Celtic striker Joe Craig, a Scottish international, and bringing former Sheffield United forward Alan Birchenall to the club on a free transfer. However, within two days of the double signing, Iley was dismissed and the team put in the control of John Pickering. Though he failed to move the club out of the relegation zone, Rovers beat Millwall 2-1 in the third round of the FA Cup before giving a very creditable display at Anfield in round four where they lost 1-0. After that, the directors decided that Pickering should lose his caretaker tag and he was given a contract until the end of the season. Unbelievably, Pickering's appointment came in the middle of an unwanted club record of 16 games without a win. During that sequence, only five points were gained, whilst the club lost vital relegation battles at home to Cardiff City (1-4) and Oldham Athletic (0-2). The run came to an end on 28 March 1979 when a Derek Fazackerley penalty gave Rovers a 1-0 win over Cambridge United.

Following the sale of Kevin Hird to Leeds United for £375,000, the most Rovers had ever received for a player at that time, Pickering paid a club record fee of £80,000 to Chelsea for Duncan McKenzie, one of the game's outstanding individualists. He also brought Mick Rathbone and Russell Coughlin from Birmingham City and Manchester City respectively in a last-ditch gamble to keep the club in Division Two. Despite these acquisitions, Rovers slumped to the foot of the table after a 3-1 home defeat by Newcastle United, a result which officially relegated them with four games still to play. Rovers ended the season with three successive victories but despite this ending, Pickering's contract was not renewed and the search for the club's fifteenth post-war manager began.

The appointment of Howard Kendall as Rovers' player-manager in June 1979 was a complete contradiction of the club's previous policy. Within a few days of taking charge at Ewood, Kendall found himself negotiating the transfer of highly-rated full-back John Bailey to Everton for £300,000. Before the start of the 1979-80 season, Kendall brought in Stafford Rangers' goalkeeper Jim Arnold, a former England semi-professional international and Stuart Parker, who was playing for Sparta Rotterdam but welcomed a return to English football. Rovers were unbeaten in their opening four games of the campaign but by mid-October were languishing near the foot of the table after winning only three of their first 14 matches. The club had also been knocked out of the League Cup, going

TONY PARKES

Sheffield-born Tony Parkes joined Blackburn Rovers from non-League Buxton and made his league debut in a 1-0 win over Swindon Town in September 1970. After failing to make much of an impression at centre-forward, manager Ken Furphy moved him back into midfield where he was able to utilise all his strengths to the full.

Parkes was an inspirational figure on the field, always working tirelessly for the good of the side. Linking up play between defence and attack, he liked nothing better than to get forward and support the forwards, scoring a number of important goals.

He helped Rovers win promotion in seasons 1974-75 and 1979-80 but sadly in 1981 his playing career was ended by a badly broken leg. Parkes, who had scored 45 goals in 391 League and Cup games, was appointed the Ewood Park club's first team coach under Bob Saxton but he had been youth and reserve-team coach for a time whilst still playing.

When Saxton was dismissed at Christmas 1986, Parkes enjoyed his first successful period as caretaker manager and though he was short-listed for the job, Don Mackay was appointed as the club's new manager. Parkes was given the position of his assistant whilst still continuing as coach. Parkes was again asked to occupy the manager's chair following the sacking of Mackay and once again turned round the team's performances on the field. Parkes was retained as first team coach when the Dalglish/Harford managerial team was appointed. He took over as the club's caretaker manager again in 1999 following the dismissal of Brian Kidd and once again his appointment saw an upturn in Rovers' fortunes. Following the appointment of Graeme Souness, Tony Parkes, who has now been at Ewood Park for over thirty years, has reverted to his role as assistant-manager.

down 6-1 at Nottingham Forest after the first meeting at Ewood Park had ended all-square at 1-1. This prompted Kendall to enter the transfer market again, bringing in Andy Crawford and Jim Branagan, both of whom were playing reserve team football for Derby County and Huddersfield Town respectively.

In the games leading up to Christmas, Rovers' league form improved and they made progress in the FA Cup, beating non-League sides in Kidderminster Harriers (Away 2-0) and Stafford Rangers (Home 2-0). On 12 January 1980, Rovers travelled to table-topping Grimsby Town and won 2-1 with Duncan McKenzie scoring both goals. It was the start of a remarkable unbeaten run which saw Rovers win 14 and draw one of their next 15 matches. The only point dropped in this sequence was at home to Exeter City and it was the Grecians who ended the unbeaten run on 12 April 1980 with a 2-0 win over Rovers at St James Park. Despite this setback, the club were not only up with the promotion pack but, having beaten First Division Coventry City 1-0, were in the fifth round of the FA Cup. Their opponents were Aston Villa, whom Rovers took to a replay before a 1-0 defeat led to their exit at Villa Park.

Following an Andy Crawford hat-trick in a 4-2 win over Reading, Rovers lost 2-1 at home to promotion rivals Sheffield Wednesday in front of an Ewood Park crowd of 26,130. It was only a minor setback as a Simon Garner goal gave the club a 1-0 win at Oxford United four days later. Promotion was finally achieved on 29 April 1980 when two goals from Andy Crawford gave Rovers a 2-1 win at Bury, though the Shakers gained revenge four days later in the final game of the season, winning by a similar scoreline!

The final placings were as follows:

	P.	W.	D.	L.	F.	A.	Pts
Grimsby Town	46	26	10	10	73	42	62
Blackburn Rovers	46	25	9	12	58	36	59
Sheffield Wednesday	46	21	16	9	81	47	58

During the close season, Kendall made two additions to his playing squad by signing Hull City's Roger De Vries and Micky Speight from Sheffield United. Andy Crawford, who was the previous season's top scor-

GLENN KEELEY

Glenn Keeley had played just five senior games for Ipswich Town when Newcastle United manager Joe Harvey paid £70,000 for him in the summer of 1974. Keeley, who had stood out in youth internationals and Ipswich Town's FA Youth Cup victory, replaced Bob Moncur at the heart of the Newcastle defence. However, following the appointment of Gordon Lee, he lost his place in the Magpies side and in August 1976, after making just 62 appearances for the Tyneside club, he was transferred to Blackburn Rovers for £30,000.

He made his Rovers' debut in a 2-1 defeat at Cardiff City, going on to be a first team regular at Ewood Park for eleven seasons.

Affectionately nicknamed 'Killer' Keeley, because of a number of reckless challenges and his brushes with authority, he went on to acquire cult status!

Manager Howard Kendall had partnered Keeley with Derek Fazackerley at the haert of the Blackburn defence, where they formed one of the best central defensive partnerships outside of the top flight. When Kendall left to become manager of Everton, he offered Keeley, who was in a contract dispute with Rovers, a loan spell and a chance to show what he could do in the First Division. Keeley played only 30 minutes for Everton, being sent-off in a derby with Liverpool!

He returned to Ewood Park and was immediately appointed captain of the club. He led Rovers to success in the Full Members' Cup of 1987 and then a few weeks later turned out in his testimonial match, which transpired to be his last appearance in a Rovers' shirt.

Keeley had scored 24 goals in 413 League and Cup games when he left to play for Oldham Athletic. Unable to give of his best on the Boundary Park plastic he joined Bolton Wanderers, but after just one season at Burnden Park, his contract was cancelled so he could pursue a commercial pilot's licence in the United States. He later returned to these shores to play non-League football for Chorley.

er with 18 goals in 36 games, scored Rovers' winner at Cardiff City on the opening day of the 1980-81 season, but he became unsettled and asked for a transfer. Despite this, Rovers won seven and drew two of their opening nine games to take them to the top of the Second Division. After losing 2-1 at Sheffield Wednesday on 7 October 1980, Rovers found the goals harder to come by and in the 13 games up until Christmas won just twice! In February 1981, Kendall let Duncan McKenzie join Tulsa Roughnecks in exchange for Viv Busby, whilst Tony Parkes broke his leg in the 1-1 home draw against Wrexham. The following month saw Noel Brotherston injured and he missed the final nine games of the season. Those nine matches produced five goalless draws and resulted in the club finishing fourth, pipped on goal difference for promotion to the top flight. Six days after coming so close to a second successive promotion, Howard Kendall agreed to return to Goodison Park as Everton's new manager. Though he had only spent two seasons at Ewood Park, he had turned Blackburn Rovers from a Third Division club into one of First Division potential.

The search for Kendall's replacement led the Rovers' board to approach Bob Saxton, the Plymouth Argyle manager. However, he was highly regarded by the Home Park directors and compensation had to be agreed between the two clubs before he was allowed to move to Ewood. Saxton's first excursion into the transfer market saw Swindon Town right-wing Ian Miller join Rovers for a fee of £60,000, but before the season got under way, Jim Arnold, who had cost the club £25,000 when signed from Stafford Rangers, followed Kendall to Everton for £200,000! Saxton moved quickly to fill the goalkeeping vacancy by paying £60,000 for the services of Southampton's Terry Gennoe. After losing 1-0 at home to Sheffield Wednesday on the opening day of the 1981-82 season, Rovers won four of their next five games and despite a shortage of goals, Saxton managed to keep the team in the promotion pack. In November 1981, Rovers signed Wolverhampton Wanderers' centre-forward Norman Bell, and though over the course of the season he didn't score too many goals, he formed a promising striking partnership with Simon Garner. Another player to join Rovers around this time was Sunderland midfielder Kevin Arnott, who joined the Ewood Park club on loan. During Arnott's three month loan period, Rovers continued to push for promotion and, after beating Grimsby Town 2-0 on 13 March 1982, were in third place.

NOEL BROTHERSTON

Former Northern Ireland schoolboy international Noel Brotherston began his career with Tottenham Hotspur but wasn't given much of a chance at White Hart Lane, making only one appearance before being released on a free transfer and joining Blackburn in the summer of 1977.

After making his debut in a 1-1 draw at Notts County on the opening day of the 1977-78 season, the prematurely balding Brotherston proved to be a revelation, ending the campaign as the club's leading scorer with 11 goals. One of the trickiest wingers outside of the First Division, Brotherston won the first of 27 full caps for Northern Ireland when he played against Scotland in 1980. He was a member of the Irish squad for the 1982 World Cup Finals in Spain, although the form of Norman Whiteside meant that Brotherston was restricted to substitute appearances during the competition.

A player who relied on skill and trickery, he suffered from a series of injuries and a loss of form towards the end of his career at Ewood Park, so much so that he was absent when Rovers won the Full Members' Cup in 1987. He had scored 46 goals, many of them spectacular, in 364 League and Cup games when Don Mackay released him in the summer of 1987.

Brotherston joined Bury and had one good season with the Shakers before going on loan to League newcomers, Scarborough and then the Swedish club, Motola. In 1989-90, he signed for non-League Chorley but appeared in only one game for the Victory Park club.

Brotherston became a painter and decorator but sadly died of a heart attack in 1995.

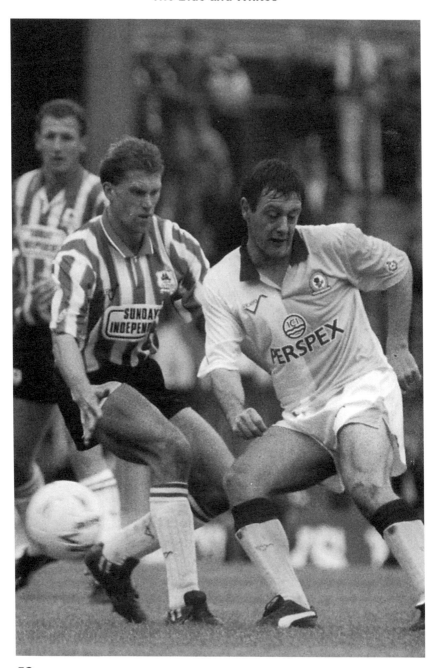

SIMON GARNER

Simon Garner broke into the Rovers' first team when the club were struggling for Second Division survival. Originally he was used in midfield but during the promotion campaign of 1979-80, manager Howard Kendall successfully converted him to inside-forward, where he formed a great partnership with Andy Kennedy for the last third of that season. It was during Kendall's reign as manager that Garner almost joined Halifax Town but fortunately for Rovers, he was reluctant to move on.

When Bob Saxton replaced Kendall, Garner seemed to find a new lease of life, his pace and power making him a handful for the Second Division defences. He capitalised on many defensive errors, notably mis-timed back passes that many defenders rued.

In 1982-83 he scored 22 league goals - it was his best return. On 10 September 1983 he scored all five goals as Rovers beat Derby County 5-1, and hit another hat-trick towards the end of the season as Rovers beat Portsmouth 4-1 at Fratton Park.

During the 1980s, Garner was recognised as one of the deadliest marksmen outside of the top flight. At the start of the 1986-87 season he scored four goals as Blackburn beat Sunderland 6-1. Another hat-trick followed on 3 September 1988 as Rovers beat Lancashire neighbours Oldham Athletic 3-1.

He established a goalscoring record for Rovers that season, taking his aggregate total to 144 goals to overhaul the record set by Tommy Briggs of 140 league goals between 1952 and 1958. The record came in the match against Manchester City when the Boston-born striker netted a hat-trick in a 4-0 win. It remained a mystery why no First Division club came in for him.

Having come close to promotion for a number of years, the club finally made it in 1991-92, Simon Garner remaining loyal to Rovers until his transfer to West Bromwich Albion in 1992, where his goalscoring exploits continued to prove valuable, taking the Baggies to the play-offs and eventually the First Division. Garner later ended his league career with Wycombe Wanderers.

However, following Arnott's return to Roker Park, results fell away, Rovers winning just two of the remaining ten games to end the season in tenth place.

In the summer of 1982, Saxton returned to his former club and paid £40,000 for the services of midfielder Colin Randell, whilst also signing Torquay United 'keeper Vince O'Keefe as cover for Terry Gennoe. Kevin Arnott, who had spent an impressive loan period at Ewood Park in 1981-82, had left Sunderland to play for Sheffield United, but on being unable to settle at Bramall Lane, joined Rovers for another loan spell. Unfortunately his second loan period with the club was not as successful as the first and, with Colin Randell having a disappointing campaign, only Simon Garner, with 22 goals in 40 league games, posed any threat to the opposition defences. Rovers, who had a nine-match unbeaten spell during which they won 5-1 at Middlesbrough on 27 November 1982, ended the season in eleventh position.

On the opening day of the 1983-84 season, Rovers drew 2-2 with Huddersfield Town but in doing so lost the services of Norman Bell, an injury that was to end his professional career. It gave an early opportunity to former Bolton Wanderers' striker Chris Thompson and he took his chance, forming an effective partnership with Simon Garner. The Boston-born forward continued where he'd left off the previous season and on 10 September 1983 scored all Rovers' goals in a 5-1 win over Derby County. With Simon Barker and Mark Patterson running the midfield, Rovers lost just one of 21 games played between 8 October 1983 and 7 March 1984, including a spell of 16 unbeaten matches. Towards the end of the season, Simon Garner netted another hat-trick in a 4-2 win at Portsmouth but too many drawn games left Rovers in sixth place at the end of the season.

After just one victory in the opening four games of the 1984-85 season, Rovers embarked on a six-match winning sequence. With Simon Garner and Chris Thompson in such fine form, new signing Jimmy Quinn from Swindon Town had to be content with a place on the substitute's bench. The Northern Ireland international eventually opened his account for the club when midway through the game against Sheffield United he replaced the injured Simon Garner and scored twice in a 3-1 win. The following week, with Garner still injured, he scored another brace at Wolverhampton Wanderers on what was his full debut as Rovers won 3-0.

MICK RATHBONE

Popularly known as 'Basil', Rathbone was brought to Ewood Park initially on a month's loan from Birmingham City by John Pickering in February 1979 before joining the club on a permanent basis for a fee of £40,000. Although a right-back, he had to switch to the opposite flank to win a regular place in Howard Kendall's side. Despite helping the club win promotion to the Second Division in 1979-80, he found himself in and out of the Rovers' first team the following season and it wasn't until the arrival of Bob Saxton that he won a regular place.

He had just established himself when in October 1983 he broke a leg in the game at Sheffield Wednesday, but fortunately he fought his way back to full fitness and regained his place in the side for the final three games of the campaign.

A solid, reliable defender, injury also cost Rathbone his place in the Blackburn team when the Ewood Park club reached the Full Members' Cup Final at Wembley and whilst he was out of action, Rovers signed Chris Sulley from Dundee United. Unable to win back his place, Rathbone, who had scored two goals in 302 League and Cup appearances, left Ewood Park to join Preston North End for a fee of £20,000.

He later combined playing for the Deepdale club with that of organising the commercial activities of North West Counties League club, Darwen. Rathbone is still at Deepdale as the club's physiotherapist.

A Derek Fazackerley penalty at Carlisle United on 23 December 1984 gave Rovers a 1-0 win and a four-point cushion at the top of the Second Division prior to the game at Leeds United on Boxing Day. A 2-1 win over the Yorkshire club confirmed Rovers' position at the top of the table but then things began to go horribly wrong. After losing 3-1 at home to Huddersfield Town, Rovers' next three league games all ended in 1-1 draws,

JIM BRANAGAN

The son of former Manchester City and Oldham Athletic full-back, Ken Branagan, he too joined Oldham Athletic as a schoolboy before signing professional forms in the summer of 1973. Though he captained the Latics' reserve team, he couldn't break into the Boundary Park club's first team on a regular basis and had appeared in just 27 league games for them when he left to try his luck in South African football with Cape Town City. It wasn't long before he was back in England where he joined Huddersfield Town. Again he was unable to hold down a regular place with the Yorkshire club and in October 1979, Howard Kendall brought him to Ewood Park, paying Huddersfield £20,000 for his services.

Branagan soon established himself as the club's first-choice right-back and in 1979-80, helped Rovers win promotion to the Second Division. A great favourite with the Blackburn faithful, Branagan was a versatile player who could turn out in midfield as well as any of the defensive positions, though it is as Mick Rathbone's full-back partner that he is best remembered. Though he captained the side on a number of occasions, he lost his place in the Rovers' side midway through the 1986-87 season and therefore was sat on the bench during the club's appearance in the Full Members' Cup Final at Wembley.

He had scored five goals in 332 League and Cup games when he left Ewood Park to join Preston North End. He made just three appearances for the Lilywhites before joining former Rovers' boss Bob Saxton at York City where he ended his league career. He later had a spell playing non-League football for Chorley.

whilst a week later the club lost 2-0 at home to Manchester United in the fifth round of the FA Cup. Another 1-1 home draw against promotion rivals Oxford United was followed by three successive defeats, but despite the club slipping down the league, the manager was reluctant to bring in new faces, preferring to stick with the players that had taken the club to the top of the Second Division. After three more successive defeats near the end of the season, Jimmy Quinn netted a hat-trick in a 3-1 win at Sheffield United, leaving Rovers praying for a footballing miracle on the final day of the season. The Ewood Park club had to beat already relegated Wolverhampton Wanderers whilst hoping rivals Manchester City and Portsmouth both lost! Although Rovers defeated the Molineux club 3-0, Manchester City gained the points they needed to win promotion, beating Charlton Athletic 5-1 to leave Rovers in fifth place.

Rovers made a good start to the 1985-86 campaign and were unbeaten in the opening six games. However, a run of eight games without a win in the weeks leading up to Christmas left the club perilously close to the relegation zone. Results after the turn of the year didn't improve and following five successive home defeats, Third Division football looked a distinct possibility. Then on 19 April 1986, after the club had gone ten matches without a win, Rovers produced one of the shock results of the season as Mark Patterson netted a hat-trick in a 6-1 win over Sheffield United at Ewood Park. However, after losing 3-0 at Charlton Athletic the following week, Rovers took to the field for the final game of the season against Grimsby Town knowing that only a win would ensure Second Division safety. Many of the 7,600 crowd were still entering the ground when, with just 42 seconds gone, Simon Garner put Rovers in front - it was the goal poacher's 100th league goal for the club. Though the Mariners equalised, further goals from David Hamilton and Simon Barker gave Rovers a 3-1 win and the points that kept the club in the Second Division as they finished the campaign in 19th place.

Three straight wins in the opening matches of the 1986-87 season, including a 6-1 defeat of Sunderland in which Simon Garner scored four times, led Rovers' supporters to believe that the club would once again be challenging for promotion to the top flight. However, the next ten games brought two draws and eight defeats and not surprisingly the Ewood crowd began to turn against both the board and the manager. Demonstrations became a regular feature at home games during the season and after Rovers, who were just one place and one point above bottom placed Huddersfield Town when the teams met on Boxing Day, lost 2-1, Saxton was sacked as

TERRY GENNOE

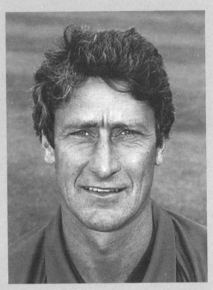

Terry Gennoe began his Football League career with Bury but in May 1975 he moved to Halifax Town where his displays soon attracted the attention of a number of top clubs. In 1978 he moved south to play for Southampton, appearing for the Saints in the 1979 League Cup Final. However, he was unable to win a regular place in the Southampton side and in August 1981 he joined Blackburn Rovers for a fee of £60,000.

A tall, commanding figure in the six-yard box, Gennoe dominated on crosses and yet, for such a big man, was exceptionally agile when coping with ground shots. His performances for Rovers led to him being selected in the 1984-85 PFA Second Division team. Despite having to overcome a series of niggling injuries and a serious viral illness during the 1986-87 season, and so missing out on the club's appearance in the Full Members' Cup Final, Gennoe went on to create a new appearance record for goalkeepers.

When Vince O'Keefe broke his leg in the fifth game of the 1987-88 season, Gennoe was restored to first team action and seemed to get better with every game he played for the Ewood Park club. Sadly, injuries began to catch up with him and he made his final league appearance, his 289th, in the first match of the 1990-91 season. Gennoe continued to play for the club's Central League side but, following the arrival of Bobby Mimms in December 1991 and continual problems with a knee injury, he decided to retire at the end of the 1991-92 season.

Gennoe remained at Ewood Park as a member of the club's coaching staff but is now Rovers' Education Officer.

manager. The directors asked Tony Parkes to take charge of team affairs on a temporary basis and during the five games he was at the helm, Rovers won two and drew three!

The club's next manager was Don Mackay, who joined Rovers from the backroom staff of Glasgow Rangers. Gradually the club began to climb up the table but it was in the Full Members' Cup that Mackay and Rovers were to make their mark.

The competition had only been introduced the previous season but Rovers had been one of a number of First and Second Division clubs to ignore it. After a change of heart, Rovers travelled to Huddersfield Town for what was to be the club's only away tie in the competition. Goals from Brotherston and Quinn were enough to beat the Terriers 2-1 on a freezing cold night at Leeds Road. A Simon Garner goal gave Rovers a 1-0 win over Sheffield United in round two and a place in the third round where their opponents were Oxford United. Simon Garner scored the only goal of the first-half in this seven-goal thriller against First Division opposition. Two goals early in the second-half put the visitors into the lead but Glenn Keeley popped up to equalise. Whitehurst scored again for Oxford but Rovers wouldn't lie down and Simon Barker equalised from the penalty-spot after Scott Sellars had been brought down. With just three minutes remaining, Ainscow and Miler were brought on. Miller made ground and crossed for Ainscow to score with a brilliant diving header - his one and only touch of the game! In the quarter-final, Rovers faced holders Chelsea but after a goalless first-half, Curry, Garner and Miller all found the net to give the Ewood Park club a comprehensive 3-0 victory. By the time Ipswich Town visited Ewood Park for the semi-final, Rovers had not only acquired two new faces in Colin Hendrey and Chris Sulley but had also pulled away from the relegation zone. After an edgy start, Rovers settled down to play some good football and ran out easy winners 3-0. It would be impossible to over-estimate the importance of the occasion of the final to Blackburn Rovers and their supporters. For not only did it give the club a chance to rescue a disappointing season but it also offered the opportunity to lay to rest the ghost of the FA Cup Final some twenty-seven years earlier.

Full Members' Cup Final 1987: Blackburn Rovers 1 Charlton Athletic 0

The game itself was almost a non-event. Vince O'Keefe, the Rovers' number two goalkeeper, became an instant hero as he made a number of fine saves to keep Blackburn in the game. With the prospect of extra-time looming, Ian Miller's perfect cross to the far side of the penalty area tempted Bob Bolder, the Charlton 'keeper, off his line but he could only get his fingertips to the ball and as a result it fell invitingly to Colin Hendrey. The big, blond striker sent in a superb angled shot off the inside of the near post and into the net for the only goal of the game. The cup was presented to Glenn Keeley, who made his only mistake of the day and dropped it!

On the Monday evening, the team returned to the town for a civic reception and were given an ecstatic welcome by thousands of fans. For a brief moment, the burden of Rovers' past glories had been lifted as at last the Blackburn public had something to celebrate.

Having ended the 1986-87 season in 12th place, manager Don Mackay added to the Ewood Park playing staff by bringing in Nicky Reid from Manchester City, Howard Gayle from Stoke City and Scottish international defender Ally Dawson from Glasgow Rangers. Unfortunately the new faces didn't bring any immediate success and after only three wins in the opening ten games of the 1987-88 campaign, Rovers fans were beginning to get a little disgruntled. However, on 30 September 1987, Rovers embarked on a 23-match unbeaten run which lifted the club to the top of the Second Division. In the middle of this run, Rovers' manager Don Mackay persuaded Barcelona to part with former Tottenham Hotspur and Scottish international Steve Archibald and he arrived at Ewood Park on loan until the end of the season. Although he didn't get on the scoresheet on his debut as Rovers beat Birmingham City 2-0, he netted twice in the 3-2 win at league leaders Aston Villa, a result which saw the Ewood Park club leapfrog over the Villans into top spot. After the unbeaten run came to an end on 5 March 1988 following Rovers' 2-1 defeat at Stoke City, results started to go against the club and with just eight games of the season left, Mackay, with the help of Steve Archibald, persuaded former Argentinian World Cup star Ossie Ardilles to join Rovers. Sadly, the gamble appeared to have failed when on his debut in a 3-0 defeat at Plymouth Argyle, Ardilles was injured by a late tackle from Nicky Marker, later to become a Blackburn player himself! With Ardilles out of the side, Rovers dropped crucial points over the Easter period and with just four games to play, found themselves in fifth place, four points behind leaders Millwall. Yet, if Rovers could win

IAN MILLER

Flying Scot Ian Miller began his career with Bury in 1973, but after just twelve months at Gigg Lane he joined Nottingham Forest before being allowed to move to Doncaster Rovers in 1975. Three years later he moved to Swindon Town, where he quickly established himself as one of the lower division's most dangerous attacking wingers. He had scored nine goals in 127 league games for the Robins when Rovers' manager Bob Saxton paid £60,000 to bring him to Ewood Park.

He soon became a great favourite with the Rovers' fans - an orthodox winger with great pace, he liked nothing better than to get to the dead-ball line and put in a telling cross. As well as his attcaking role, Miller worked hard on the right-side of midfield, providing valuable defensive cover for the club's full-back. Probably the highlight of Miller's eight seasons at Ewood Park was his contribution in the club's successful Full Members' Cup Final when his run and cross provided Colin Hendrey with the game's only goal.

Though his first team appearances became more limited over the next couple of seasons, he remained an invaluable player to have on the bench, though he did find himself restored to the first team for a lengthy spell towards the end of the 1988-89 season.

At the end of that campaign, during which he had acted as club captain, Miller, who had scored 17 goals in 293 League and Cup games, was allowed to continue his career with newly promoted Port Vale, where, after hanging up his boots, he became involved in coaching the Valiants after a spell as the Vale Park club's Community Scheme organiser.

all of their remaining games they would end the season as Second Division champions! However, following a goalless home draw against Swindon Town and a defeat at Crystal Palace, Rovers then drew 1-1 at home to Reading, leaving them needing to win their final match at already-crowned champions Millwall to make the play-offs! Against all the odds, Rovers, for whom Simon Garner scored twice, won 4-1. Having finished in fifth place, Rovers faced Chelsea in a two-legged semi-final tie. Unfortunately two second-half mistakes by David Mail gifted the visitors two goals to take back to the second-leg at Stamford Bridge which Chelsea won easily 4-1.

The failure to win promotion meant the end of the loan periods of Archibald and Ardilles, whilst others to leave Ewood Park included Chris Price to Aston Villa for £150,000 and Simon Barker, who left to join Queen's Park Rangers for £400,000. His midfield partner Mark Patterson also left Rovers, joining neighbours Preston North End for £20,000. The replacements included full-back Mark Atkins, who cost £45,000 from Scunthorpe United, and Andy Kennedy from Birmingham City for £50,000.

Rovers made a very good start to the 1988-89 season, winning five and drawing one of their first six games, with Simon Garner netting a hat-trick in a 3-1 home win over Oldham Athletic. With Howard Gayle also finding his shooting boots, Rovers were again able to challenge for promotion. After the turn of the year, Rovers embarked on an eight-match unbeaten run, but by the time Manchester City visited Ewood Park on 15 April 1989, Rovers were in third place some 11 points behind the Maine Road club, who were second. A crowd of 16,927, easily the season's highest, were at Ewood Park to see Andy Kennedy give Rovers a seventh-minute lead, which was extended six minutes later as Garner equalled Tommy Briggs' record of 140 league goals for the club. In the 74th minute, Garner scored his second and Rovers' third goal to claim the club goalscoring record for himself. Three minutes later he completed his hat-trick to give Rovers a 4-0 win. Three wins in the last five games of the season gave Rovers a place in the play-offs for the second successive season after they had again ended the campaign in fifth place. Despite being held at home to a goalless draw by Watford in the first-leg of the play-off semi-finals, a Simon Garner goal was enough to earn Rovers a 1-1 draw at Vicarage Road and a place in the play-off final on the away-goals rule. An Ewood Park

SIMON BARKER

A product of the Ewood Park club's youth development scheme, Farnworth-born midfielder Simon Barker worked his way up through the club's ranks before making his League debut at Swansea City in October 1983.

Barker proved to be an excellent reader of the game and soon became noted for his runs into the opposition penalty area, which brought him a number of important goals. His form for Rovers, which helped take the club to the brink of promotion to the First Division, led to him winning selection for the England Under-21 team. He was a member of the Blackburn side that defeated Charlton Athletic to win the Full Members' Cup Final in 1987 but the following season, his last at Ewood Park, he was plagued by injuries. He had scored 41 goals in 208 first team games for Rovers when the club received a record fee of £400,000 from Queen's Park Rangers for him.

Initially he found it difficult to break into the first team at Loftus Road, but once he settled down he began to develop a formidable midfield partnership with England international Ray Wilkins.

Barker stayed at Loftus Road for ten seasons, scoring 41 goals in 376 games before being released in the early part of the 1998-99 season. He joined Port Vale on trial before securing a full-time contract with the Valiants. On his return to his old club, he scored his first goal for Vale. Though not as quick as he used to be, Simon Barker still possesses an excellent football brain.

crowd of 16,421 saw Howard Gayle score twice in the first-leg of the play-off final as Rovers beat Crystal Palace 3-1. He had the opportunity of net-ting a hat-trick but sadly missed from the penalty-spot! In the second-leg at Selhurst Park, Rovers gave what was probably their most disappointing dis-play of the season, losing 3-0 to Palace after extra-time.

During the close season, Rovers' manager Don Mackay captured the national headlines when he signed former Manchester United and Republic of Ireland internationals Frank Stapleton and Kevin Moran from France and Spain respectively. These two experienced campaigners helped Rovers

DAVID MAIL

Bristol-born David Mail was a member of Aston Villa's FA Youth Cup winning side of 1980, but after failing to break through into the club's first team, he left Villa Park in January 1982 to join Blackburn Rovers, primarily as cover for the first team centre-halves Derek Fazackerley and Glenn Keeley. With the former player coming towards the end of his long Ewood Park career, Mail was promoted to play along-side Keeley. Following Keeley's departure in the summer of 1987, Mail struck up an  impressive central defensive partnership with Colin Hendrey. Though not as big as the majority of players in his position, Mail proved to be more than capable in the air, whilst his speed and strong-tackling made him quite a formidable opponent.

Mail was a member of Blackburn's side that won the Full Members' Cup Final in 1987 and appeared in the club's three disappointing play-off campaigns. After surprisingly losing his place in the heart of the Rovers' defence to Keith Hill, he fought his way back to partner David May. However, after scoring four goals in 231 League and Cup games, Mail moved to Hull City in the summer of 1990 for a fee of £160,000.

Despite a spate of injuries during his time at Boothferry Park, Mail appeared in 169 first team games for the Tigers before being released at the end of the 1994-95 season.

to win four and draw six of their opening ten league games of the 1989-90 season, with Simon Garner netting a hat-trick in a 5-0 home win over Barnsley. Shortly after the club suffered their first league defeat of the season at Newcastle United. Colin Hendrey, who had been in dispute with the club, left to play for Manchester City, joining the Maine Road club for a fee of £700,000. Though Rovers turned in a number of disappointing displays, the club ended the season in fifth place for the third successive campaign and so qualified for the play-offs again. Unfortunately Rovers' opponents in the semi-final were Swindon Town, who were led by Ossie Ardilles. They returned to Wiltshire with a 2-1 lead from the first-leg. A crowd of 12.416 crammed into the County Ground but a similar scoreline meant that the Ewood club faced another season of Second Division football.

After three unsuccessful promotion campaigns, Rovers failed to address the problem of an ageing team prior to the start of the 1990-91 season. Leading goalscorere Simon Garner and chief playmaker Scott Sellars both required hernia operations, whilst the close season acquisitions of veteran Mike Duxbury and Lee Richardson, in an exchange deal which took Andy Kennedy to Watford, were inadequate.

Rovers, who lost four of their opening five games, weren't helped by the fact that eight first team players missed three or more months football over the course of the season. Home defeats over Christmas at the hands of Notts County (0-1) and Oxford United (1-3) left the club perilously close to the foot of the Second Division. In the FA Cup, Rovers almost beat Liverpool in front of an Ewood Park crowd of 18,524. Only a last-minute own goal by Mark Atkins kept the Reds in the competition. Unfortunately Rovers lost 3-0 in the replay at Anfield. Three days after their exit from the FA Cup, Rovers travelled to Newcastle United but a 1-0 defeat left them in 20th place, just four points ahead of bottom club, Hull City. With just one win in their last ten games, the future didn't look bright.

It was then that an interest in the club was acquired by multi-millionaire Jack Walker. His injection of a million pounds spent on goalkeeper Bobby Mimms (£250,000 from Tottenham Hotspur) and the Coventry pair of Steve Livingstone and Tony Dobson, who cost £750,000, was perhaps the single most important event in allowing Rovers to escape relegation as they finished in 19th place.

During the summer of 1991, Rovers signed full-back Stuart Munro

COLIN HENDREY

Colin Hendrey was playing for Dundee when Rovers' manager Don Mackay brought him to Ewood Park for a fee of £30,000 in March 1989. The Scottish club had a few reservations about letting Hendrey come south of the border and insisted that they receive half of any subsequent transfer fee.

He made his debut as a replacement for Glenn Keeley in the Full Members' Cup match against Ipswich Town, and when Keeley was restored to the side, he was moved to lead the attack. It was in this position that he endeared himself to Rovers' fans when he scored the only goal of the Full Members' Cup Final win over Charlton Athletic.

When Keeley left Ewood Park, Hendrey was given the number five shirt. His performances led to a number of top clubs following his progress and in November 1989, after having been left out of the team following a contractual dispute, he left Rovers to join Manchester City for £700,000.

A great favourite at Maine Road, he was the club's first-choice centre-half until the arrival of Keith Curle, when he left to return to Ewood Park. Under the guidance of Blackburn's new manager, Kenny Dalglish, Hendrey became a much more polished defender than he had been during his first spell with the club.

His performances led to him winning the first of 35 Scottish caps, whom he later captained during the 1998 World Cup in France.

Hendrey was outstanding during Rovers' Premier League Championship-winning season of 1994-95, scoring crucial goals at Aston Villa and Leeds United. Not surprisingly, he was selected for the PFA Premier League team of the year.

Hendrey continued to display the last-ditch tackles and brave headers at Ewood Park until 1998 when, after scoring 34 goals in 384 League and Cup games in his two spells with the club, he left to play for Glasgow Rangers.

After an unhappy time at Ibrox Park, he returned to Premier League action with Coventry City.

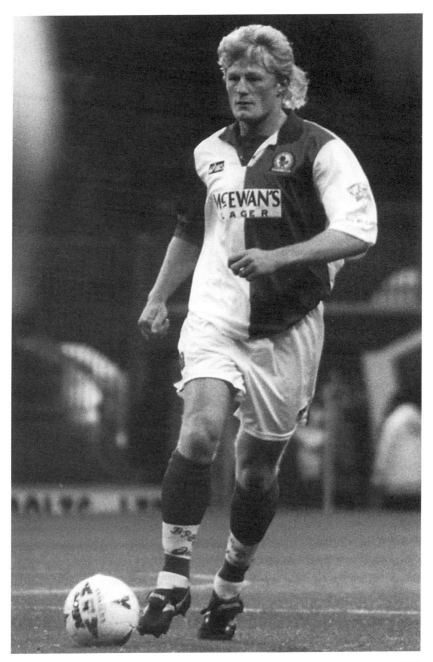

SCOTT SELLARS

After graduating through the ranks at Leeds United, midfielder Scott Sellars made his League debut for the Yorkshire club in a goalless draw at Shrewsbury Town on the final day of the 1982-83 season. After asking for a transfer he was sold to Blackburn Rovers for £20,000 in July 1986 and won a Full Members' Cup Final medal at the end of his first season with Rovers.

In 1987-88 he was capped by England Under-21 against Scotland, France and Sweden. Though he was plagued by injuries in 1990-91, he returned to feature prominently in Rovers' Second Division promotion campaign in 1991-92. Having helped the club climb into the newly formed Premier League, Sellars, who had scored 41 goals in 245 first team games, was allowed to return to Elland Road for a fee of £800,000.

It proved to be an unhappy move and after only seven Premier League games for Leeds, he dropped into the First Division to join Newcastle United. However, he soon made a quick return to the top flight, helping the Magpies win the First Division Championship in 1992-93.

In December 1995, Sellars, who had scored seven goals in 71 games for the St James' Park club, was on the move again, this time to Bolton Wanderers for £750,000. Though he failed to stop the Trotters crashing out of the Premier League, he was instrumental in their First Division Championship-winning season of 1996-97, his performances winning him a number of man-of-the-match awards.

After that, injuries began to take their toll on the left-sided midfielder and in the summer of 1999, after scoring 16 goals in 125 League and Cup games for the Trotters, he was surprisingly released and joined Huddersfield Town.

74

from Glasgow Rangers and spent £750,000 on securing the services of Barnsley midfielder Steve Agnew. On the eve of the campaign, Mackay finally signed the forward he wanted when David Speedie arrived at Ewood Park in a £500,000 deal from Liverpool.

However, Rovers made a very disappointing start to the 1991-92 season, taking just one point from the opening three games and making a first round League Cup exit at the hands of Third Division Hull City. Agnew, the club's record signing, was injured in the second leg of the tie at Boothferry Park and never played for the club again! These results led to the sacking of Don Mackay, though at the time of his departure, the board placed on record their appreciation of all the work that he had done.

Tony Parkes was again put in temporary charge and, with David Speedie scoring a number of vital goals, the club began to move up the table. Rovers won four and drew two of the seven games whilst Parkes was in charge, but as he prepared Rovers for the home match against Plymouth Argyle on 12 October 1991, the Blackburn board announced that they had persuaded Kenny Dalglish to end his self-imposed retirement and he became the club's 18th post-war manager. Also Ray Harford, the former Luton Town and Wimbledon boss, had agreed to join the club as assistant-manager. Tony Parkes was installed as Rovers' first-team coach. Within a couple of weeks of taking charge, Dalglish began to spend some of the money that Jack Walker had made available to him, splashing out £500,000 on Blackpool full-back Alan Wright and £700,000 on former Blackburn favourite Colin Hendrey from Manchester City. After a 2-0 win at Charlton Athletic, Dalglish paid the club's first seven-figure fee - £1.1 million - for the services of Everton forward Mike Newell and he scored on his debut in a 3-0 win over Barnsley. Another mid-season signing, and possibly the most important, was that of experienced campaigner Gordon Cowans, who joined Rovers from Aston Villa. Following a 3-1 victory over Oxford United at the beginning of December 1991, the club's chairman Bill Fox, a lifelong Rovers' supporter, passed away. As the season unfolded new players continued to arrive at Ewood Park in the shape of Chris Price (Aston Villa), Tim Sherwood (Norwich City) and the exciting Roy Wegerle (Queen's Park Rangers).

After four successive wins at the start of February 1992, Rovers won only one of their next 13 league games, a sequence that coincided with the

MARK ATKINS

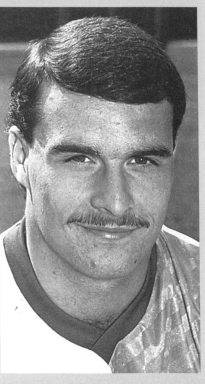

England Schoolboy international Mark Atkins began his Football League career with Scunthorpe United and had appeared in 66 League and Cup games when Blackburn Rovers paid £45,000 for his services in the summer of 1988. Like his predecessor, Chris Price, Atkins developed an eye for goal and, under Don Mackay, was the club's first-choice right-back as Rovers challenged for promotion to the top flight. However, as the club's fortunes took a turn for the worse, Atkins found himself in and out of the Rovers' side. The following season, caretaker manager Tony Parkes moved Atkins into a midfield role and this was continued by Kenny Dalglish as Rovers reached the Premier League via the play-offs.

Though he didn't always make the starting line-up during Rovers' first season in the Premier League, Atkins' versatility made him an important member of the Blackburn squad. After helping Rovers win the Premier League Championship in 1994-95, Atkins, who had scored 40 goals in 312 games, left the Ewood Park club to join Wolverhampton Wanderers for a fee of £1 million.

Booked on his debut against Luton Town, he was moved from mid-field to the sweeper position during the 1996-97 season with great effect before being restored to a more forward position. He has continued to show his versatility and in 1997-98 captained the club in a number of games during Keith Curle's absence. He went on to score ten goals in 151 League and Cup games for the Molineux club before being released in the summer of 1999.

76

KEVIN MORAN

Kevin Moran has the dubious distinction of being the first player ever to be sent-off in an FA Cup Final when he up-ended Everton's Peter Reid in the 1985 showpiece. United went on to win 1-0 and, though it meant he wasn't officially eligible for a medal, the FA relented following an appeal. It was Moran's second medal, having picked one up in the 1983 Final against Brighton. Moran, who had joined United from Irish club Pegasus was as tough a tackler as any in the Football League, this causing him to experience more than his fair share of injuries. He won his first international honour with the Republic of Ireland in 1980 when he played against Switzerland. After appearing in 288 games for the Reds, he left Old Trafford in the 1988 close season to join Sporting Gijon in the Spanish League.

He returned to England in January 1990 to join Blackburn Rovers. A great favourite with the Ewood Park faithful, he captained the team to play-off success at Wembley in 1991-92. Indeed, Rovers may well

have not been there if his brave headed goal hadn't accounted for Derby County in the semi-final of the play-offs.

During the club's first season in the Premier League, Moran's ability to read the game and organise the defence proved invaluable. Despite suffering a number of horrific facial injuries, Moran continued to give total commitment to the Rovers' cause until the summer of 1994, when, after scoring 12 goals in 173 first team games, he decided to retire and concentrate on the sports promotion business he runs with former Manchester United team-mate Jesper Olsen.

absence of Mike Newell, who had been injured in the 3-1 defeat of Newcastle United on 15 February, a match in which David Speedie netted a hat-trick. Newell returned to first team action in mid-April, scoring in a 2-2 draw at Tranmere Rovers. After beating Millwall 2-1 and drawing 2-2 with Sunderland, Rovers travelled to Plymouth Argyle on the final day of the season needing to win to clinch a place in the play-offs. The Pilgrims also needed to win to avoid relegation to the Third Division! Despite going a goal behind after just 12 minutes, David Speedie netted his second hat-trick of the season to give Rovers a 3-1 win and a spot in the play-offs. Speedie's total of 23 goals was Rovers' highest individual tally in the Football League since Andy McEvoy's 29 goals in 1964-65.

Rovers' opponents in the two-legged semi-finals were Derby County who, though they finished four points ahead of the Ewood Park club, had been beaten by Blackburn in both league games. Goals from Gabbiadini and Johnson gave the Rams a 2-0 lead inside the first quarter-of-an-hour but Rovers settled down and by half-time had drawn level courtesy of strikes by Scott Sellars and Mike Newell. In the second-half, two goals from David Speedie helped Rovers win 4-2, a lead that they had to defend at the Baseball Ground three days later. Despite going down 2-1, Rovers won 5-4 on aggregate to claim their place in the play-off final against Leicester City on the Spring Bank Holiday Monday.

Second Division Play-Off Final: Blackburn Rovers 1 Leicester City 0

A Wembley crowd of 68,147 saw a fairly even first-half but as the interval approached, Leicester's captain Steve Walsh clashed with David Speedie in the penalty area. Referee George Courtney, who was officiating in his final match as a Football League referee, had no doubts that the Blackburn striker had been impeded and awarded Rovers a penalty. With the last kick of the first-half, Mike Newell sent Leicester 'keeper Carl Muggleton the wrong way to give Rovers the lead. Not surprisingly, the Foxes applied a lot of pressure in the second-half, but late in the game Rovers were awarded a second penalty when Mark Atkins was upended in the area. This time Muggleton saved Newell's spot-kick and though Leicester pushed hard for an equaliser, Rovers hung on for a memorable victory.

JASON WILCOX

Left-winger Jason Wilcox worked his way through the ranks at Blackburn to make his Football League debut against Swindon Town in April 1990. However, it wasn't until the 1991-92 season that he established himself as a first team regular, though many of his games were on the right-hand side of midfield owing to the fine form of Scott Sellars.

Sadly, injury prevented him from playing any part in the play-off matches which saw Rovers promoted to the Premier League.

Following Sellars' departure to Leeds United in the summer of 1992, Wilcox claimed the left-wing position as his own and went on to have an impressive first season in the top flight. Wilcox's career was thrown into doubt during the summer of 1993 after he had contracted Legionnaires' Disease and was out of action for a good number of weeks. However, he returned in December 1993 and towards the end of that season, his form was such that he had won selection to the England squad, eventually making his full debut against Hungary in 1996 when he made an outstanding contribution in a 3-0 success. After that, his progress with Rovers was hampered by a series of operations, including one to move remove gristle from his knee, but he recovered to take his place in the Rovers' side.

Wilcox, who was continually shuffled from wide left to left-back, often in the game itself, was forced to miss the first half of the 1998-99 season through a hernia operation. New manager Brian Kidd made him the on-field captain but at the end of that season, in which he had taken his tally of goals to 34 in 286 League and Cup games, he was transferred to Leeds United.

The Blue and Whites

The celebrations at Wembley were repeated the following day as thousands of supporters lined the streets of Blackburn to cheer on the team as they were driven to the Town Hall in an open-topped bus.

Having gained promotion to the newly-formed Premier League, Rovers signed Middlesbrough winger Stuart Ripley for £1.2 million and then smashed the British transfer record by paying £3.3 million for Southampton's highly-rated centre-forward Alan Shearer. Unfortunately for Rovers fans, the Saints insisted that cult-hero David Speedie join the south coast club as part of the deal.

Rovers wasted little time in making an impact on the title race. By the beginning of October, the Ewood Park club had triumphed in seven of their 11 games, led the table by a point and had the league's top marksman in Alan Shearer, who had found the net 11 times in 11 games. On 3 October 1992, Rovers disposed of league leaders Norwich City 7-1, Shearer scored two and made four others as Blackburn produced an emphatic triumph. By the end of November, Rovers were joint second in the table, having been knocked off the perch by Norwich, but Shearer had taken his goal tally to 16. At Christmas Rovers were again flirting with the title, moving into second spot with a 3-1 defeat of the previous season's champions Leeds United. Shearer again collected two more goals, his tally now standing at 22, when disaster struck. Shearer injured his knee during the Christmas programme and exacerbated the knock in the League Cup tie against Cambridge United. The injury was to prove far more serious than at first feared and the England striker didn't appear for Rovers again that season. His place in the side was taken by Roy Wegerle but Rovers' league form began to suffer. The club's FA Cup ambitions were ended in the fifth round by Sheffield United and their League Cup campaign ended at the semi-final stage when they were emphatically beaten 6-3 on aggregate by Sheffield Wednesday. In a bid to keep the season alive, the Rovers' manager signed Graeme Le Saux from Chelsea in a £650,000 deal which saw Steve Livingstone move to Stamford Bridge, whilst Roy Wegerle was used as part of the deal that saw Coventry's Kevin Gallacher arrive at Ewood Park in a £1.5 million package.

A late rally towards the end of the season, during which Rovers won eight of their final ten games, meant that the club never slipped out of contention for a place in Europe, although ultimately that was denied them by a Norwich side that ended the campaign an agonising point ahead of Rovers, who ended the season in fourth place.

Despite facing the prospect of beginning the 1993-94 season without the injured Alan Shearer, Blackburn manager Kenny Dalglish resisted the temptation to spend more of Jack Walker's millions. The first four games brought nine points and in the fifth, Shearer went on as a substitute and scored in a 1-1 draw against Newcastle United.

In September 1993, Dalglish entered the transfer market, signing the versatile Paul Warhurst from Sheffield Wednesday for £2.3 million. In October, England midfielder David Batty moved from Leeds United also for £2.3 million, whilst a month later Dalglish splashed out £2.4 million for Southampton's Tim Flowers - now the most expensive goalkeeper in Britain.

A 3-3 draw at Leeds United in October 1993 brought the first hat-trick for Alan Shearer since his arrival at Ewood Park and moved Rovers into sixth place in the Premiership. They continued to pick up points regularly and though by Christmas the club had moved up to third position, they were still some 14 points behind leaders Manchester United. On Boxing Day, Rovers visited Old Trafford and were unlucky to come away with only a point after a last-minute equaliser by Paul Ince. The club's run in the League Cup ended with a 1-0 defeat in the fourth round at Tottenham Hotspur and a shock third round exit from the FA Cup also looked likely as Portsmouth fought out a deserved 3-3 draw at Ewood Park. However, after Rovers had won the replay 3-1 they again fell in the fourth round, losing to First Division Charlton Athletic in a replay.

Attention now turned towards the league and when Shearer scored twice in a 3-1 home win over Swindon Town in March, Rovers were just three points behind United. There seemed a real possibility that the champions could be caught - something thought unlikely in December. But a disastrous 4-1 defeat at Wimbledon in the next game dented Rovers' confidence and robbed them of the chance to go clear at the top!

Rovers responded in dramatic fashion by beating Manchester United 2-0 at home at the start of April with two goals by that man Shearer. A 1-0 home win over Aston Villa nine days later put Rovers level on points though United had a game in hand. Unfortunately, Rovers stuttered in the run-in, taking just five points from the final five matches and had to settle

MIKE NEWELL

Formerly a Liverpool junior, he was not offered terms at Anfield and made his Football League debut whilst on trial with Crewe Alexandra. Failing to impress manager Dario Gradi, he moved on to Wigan Athletic, where he scored one of the goals in the club's 3-1 Freight Rover Trophy success over Brentford at Wembley in 1985.

Newell went on to score 35 goals in 92 games for the Latics before being transferred to First Division Luton Town in January 1986. In 1986-87 he was ever-present and the Hatters leading scorer with 12 goals. Shortly afterwards he was signed by Leicester City for a club record £350,000 and in two seasons at Filbert Street hardly missed a match, ending the 1988-89 season as the Foxes' top scorer. In the summer of 1989 he joined Everton for £1.1 million but, after struggling to score goals, found himself in and out of the side.

In November 1991, he became the first player to cost Blackburn Rovers a million pounds when he accepted an offer from Kenny Dalglish to join the Ewood Park club. He scored on his debut against Barnsley and soon became a great favourite with the Blackburn fans. Despite breaking his leg in the match against Newcastle United in February 1992, he returned for the end of the season and, after scoring a vital goal in the first leg of the semi-final play-offs against Derby County, converted the penalty in the final against Leicester City that gave Rovers a 1-0 win and a place in the Premier League. Forming an effective striking partnership with Alan Shearer, he went on to score 42 goals in 157 League and Cup games before joining Birmingham City for £775,000 in July 1996.

Unable to settle at St Andrew's he had loan spells with West Ham United and Bradford City before joining Aberdeen for £160,000 in the summer of 1997. He later signed for Crewe Alexandra on a free transfer and then joined Blackpool.

for the runners-up spot. However, this meant that the following season would see European football at Ewood Park for the first time in the club's history. Alan Shearer ended the season with 31 league goals and not surprisingly was voted Footballer of the Year by the Football Writers' Association.

During the close season, David May, who had been in dispute with the club over his contract, opted to leave Ewood Park to join Manchester United, whilst Republic of Ireland international Kevin Moran announced his retirement from the game. However, Rovers again broke the British transfer record when they paid £5 million to bring Norwich City's England Under-21 international Chris Sutton to Ewood Park.

Prior to the start of the 1994-95 season, Rovers appeared in the FA Charity Shield. This was because of Manchester United's double-winning season which had brought both Premiership and FA Cup trophies to Old Trafford. The title race was always expected to be between Rovers and United and it was the reigning champions who fired the first shot with a 2-0 victory in the Charity Shield.

Alan Shearer missed a penalty on the opening day of the season against his old club Southampton but he did score Rovers' goal in a 1-1 draw. Rovers were unbeaten in their opening seven games, with new signing Chris Sutton netting a hat-trick in a 4-0 home win over Coventry City. On 15 October 1994, Rovers climbed to second place in the Premiership with a 3-2 win over Liverpool at Ewood Park. Unfortunately, by this time, Rovers' interest in Europe had come to an end after they lost 3-2 on aggregate to the part-timers of Trelleborgs. On 23 October 1994, Rovers entertained Manchester United but a series of diabolical refereeing decisions meant that the Reds maintained the upper hand in their meetings with a 4-2 win. Rovers responded by putting together a devastating seven-match winning run, including a 4-0 defeat of Queen's Park Rangers in which Alan Shearer scored a hat-trick. That result took Rovers to the top of the Premiership. League points continued to be gathered throughout the first few months of 1995 and though Rovers lost 2-1 to Newcastle United in the third round of the FA Cup, it had little effect on their form in the Premiership. At the beginning of April, Rovers won two successive away games, beating Everton 2-1 and Queen's Park Rangers 1-0, to extend their lead at the top of the table. Then, all of a sudden, with just six games to

HENNING BERG

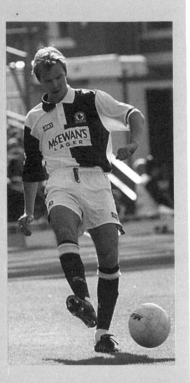

Norwegian international Henning Berg joined Blackburn Rovers from SK Lillestrom for £400,000 in January 1993 and made his debut as a substitute against Crystal Palace the following month. Although he had never played full-back prior to his arrival at Ewood Park, he emerged as one of the best attacking right-backs in the Premier League in 1993-94. When Rovers won the Premier Leagur Championship in 1994-95, Berg was one of the club's unsung heroes, a calming influence throughout the campaign. That season also saw him voted Norwegian 'Player of the Year'.

An intelligent reader of the game with a keen positional sense, Berg went on to score four goals in 185 League and Cup games for Rovers before being transferred to Manchester United in August 1997 for a fee of £5 million - a new record for a defender.

After an impressive first season for United, he played in all four World Cup games for Norway in France during the summer of 1998 as the side reached the second round before going out of the competition 1-0 to Italy.

The solid central defender had a frustrating start to the 1998-99 season when he struggled with peristent injury, but recovered to help the club win the Premier League, the FA Cup and the European Cup, where his defensive qualities came to the fore against Inter Milan at Old Trafford when an outstanding goal-line clearance denied the Italian side an away goal. Barring further injuries the Norwegian international, who has appeared 62 times for his country, could become a permanent fixture in the United side for many more seasons to come.

play Rovers began to falter. On Easter Saturday a last-minute goal gave Leeds United an undeserved point, whilst on Easter Monday Rovers went down 3-2 at home to Manchester City. Though Rovers beat Crystal Palace 2-1 three days later, a 2-0 defeat at the hands of relegation threatened West Ham United left them eight points ahead of Manchester United but the Reds had two games in hand. They duly beat Coventry City and Sheffield Wednesday to collect maximum points but Rovers kept their title hopes alive with a 1-0 home win over Newcastle United, courtesy of an Alan Shearer goal. A disputed penalty in the dying minutes of United's game at Southampton meant that Rovers had to win their final game of the season at Liverpool to take the title. If Blackburn failed to win and United claimed the three points in their match against West Ham United, the title would again go to Old Trafford. Despite Alan Shearer opening the scoring at Anfield, Rovers went down 2-1 but, within minutes of the final whistle, news filtered through that the Hammers had held Manchester United to a 1-1 draw - Rovers were champions of the Premier League.

Kenny Dalglish and Jack Walker paraded the trophy in front of the supporters as the players enjoyed a well-deserved lap of honour. The following evening the Rovers' players made a triumphant return to a packed Ewood Park where they were formally presented with the trophy.

The final placings were as follows:

	P.	W.	D.	L.	F.	A.	Pts
Blackburn Rovers	42	27	8	7	80	39	89
Manchester United	42	26	10	6	77	28	88
Nottingham Forest	42	22	11	9	72	43	77

Six weeks after guiding Rovers to the Championship, the unpredictable Dalglish was appointed director of football at Ewood Park with Ray Harford taking charge of team affairs. During the summer, Rovers' leading scorer Alan Shearer signed a thrtee-year extension to his existing contract to put an end to speculation that he might move to Italy!

The 1995-96 season saw Rovers kick-off with an Alan Shearer penalty taking all three points off Queen's Park Rangers, but then the Ewood club lost four and drew one of their next five games to slip down to 17th position in the Premiership. A 5-1 thrashing of Coventry City saw Shearer score the first of five hat-tricks during the season. A run of ten consecutive wins at Ewood Park raised the supporters' expectations but it wasn't until mid-January that an away victory was achieved when Rovers won 1-0 at Queen's Park Rangers. During this depressing run Rovers suffered a 5-0 reversal in the return match with Coventry City. The two games against Nottingham Forest saw amazing 7-0 and 5-1 victories for the Ewood Park club - the home victory in which Shearer netted a hat-trick was Blackburn's highest for 41 years and ended Forest's 25-match unbeaten run in the Premiership!

Sadly, the domestic cup competitions did little to appease the fans,

KEVIN GALLACHER

A member of a footballing family, being the grandson of the legendary Patsy Gallacher, who played for Celtic between 1911 and 1925, Kevin Gallacher began his career with Dundee United. He appeared in two Scottish Cup Finals and the UEFA Cup Final of 1987 for the Tannadice Park club before coming south of the border to join Coventry City for £900,000 in January 1990.

He was hampered by injuries during is time at Highfield Road, but it didn't deter Rovers' manager Kenny Dalglish from paying £1.5 million for his services in March 1993.

Sadly, the versatile front runner suffered an horrendous triple fracture of a leg in the match against Arsenal at Highbury in February 1994. He reappeared in the Rovers' side midway through the following season but after scoring the winning goal against Crystal Palace, ended the day with his leg back in plaster after it was broken in the same spot! Though he fought his way back to full fitness, it was 1996-97 before he won a regular place in the Blackburn side, and in the 3-1 win over Wimbledon he netted his first hat-trick for the club. In 1997-98, Gallacher had his best-ever season for the club, scoring 20 goals in all competitions, including 16 in the Premiership, including a hat-trick against Aston Villa.

The Scottish international played in all three of his country's World Cup games during the summer of 1998 and at the time of writing has appeared in more than 40 games for the Scots. Gallacher, who scored 52 goals in 161 League and Cup games for Rovers, left Ewood Park to join Newcastle United in 1999.

STUART RIPLEY

Middlesbrough-born winger Stuart Ripley began his Football League career with his home-town club before gaining further experience with a loan spell with Bolton Wanderers. On his return to Ayresome Park, he became a regular in Boro's first team and in 1986-87 helped them win promotion to the Second Division. In 1987-88 he was a key member of the Middlesbrough side that won promotion to the top flight via the play-offs. After just one season in the First Division, 'Boro were relegated to the Second Division. A virtual ever-present he helped the Teeside club win promotion to the Premier League in 1991-92, going on to score 30 goals in 290 League and Cup games before joining Blackburn Rovers for £1.3 million in July 1992.

After an impressive first season for Rovers, he won his first England cap in November 1993 when Graham Taylor selcted him for the World Cup qualifier against San Marino. He helped Rovers win the Premier League Championship in 1994-95, when he created a host of chances for the club's strikers as well as having the capacity to drop back deep to prevent opponents building up attacks. Ripley went three seasons without scoring a goal for Rovers and even lost his place to Greek international Georgios Donis. However, in 1997-98 he won back his place and gained a call up to the England team but his appearance lasted just five minutes before a torn hamstring brought his season to an end. In the summer of 1998, Ripley, who had scored 16 goals in 219 League and Cup games, was sold to Southampton for £1.5 million.

Since his arrival at The Dell, he has been troubled by a series of injuries which have restricted his number of appearances for the Saints.

Rovers going out to First Division Ipswich Town at the first hurdle in the FA Cup and Leeds United in the third round of the League Cup. Rovers' European adventure was something of a nightmare as defeats in the first three games against Spartak Moscow, Rosenborg and Legia Warsaw edged the club towards the exit. A 4-1 win over Rosenborg in the final group match saw Mike Newell score a hat-trick but, unfortunately, it was far too late to salvage a place in the knockout stage of the competition.

During the course of the season, in which Rovers finished seventh in the Premier League, Shearer became the first player to score thirty or more league goals in the top flight in three consecutive seasons and scored his 100th league goal in just 124 games with a stunning effort in the 3-2 win at Tottenham Hotspur. The famed Blackburn cheque-book was again in frequent use with ten signings being made. The most expensive capture was Garry Flitcroft from Manchester City at £3.2 million just prior to the transfer deadline. Sadly, he lasted just two minutes of his debut against Everton before being dismissed for use of an elbow!

Before the start of the 1996-97 season, Rovers, who in England striker Alan Shearer possessed the most potent goalscorer in the Premiership, found Newcastle United's offer of £15 million too good to resist. Sadly, his departure seemed to be the catalyst for further unrest at Ewood Park. The campaign began badly for Rovers with a 2-0 defeat at Ewood Park against Tottenham Hotspur on the opening day of the season, whilst their away form was a nightmare. After a 1-0 defeat at Aston Villa in their second game, Dalglish announced his departure from the club. Rovers responded positively by collecting a point at Old Trafford but just two points from the next eight games left Blackburn entrenched at the foot of the table. Ray Harford quit after only four points had been won from the opening ten games. The Blackburn board decided that they wanted a top coach to revive their fortunes and announced after a lengthy wait that the Swede Sven-Goran Eriksson would be the new man in charge at Ewood Park, once he was clear of his current contract. In the meantime, Tony Parkes was named as caretaker manager. He began the revival with a 3-0 win over Liverpool at the start of November and draws against Chelsea, Nottingham Forest and Leicester City, followed by a 2-1 defeat of Southampton, lifted Rovers out of the relegation zone. Following a 1-0 defeat at Wimbledon, Rovers lost just one of their next twelve games and

ALAN SHEARER

Although born in Newcastle, Alan Shearer signed for Southampton and made his Football League debut at Chelsea in March 1988 as a substitute a month before turning professional. In his first full league game, he caused a sensation, netting a hat-trick in a 4-2 win over Arsenal and becoming the youngest player to score three times in a First Division match.

Though he wasn't the most prolific of scorers during his time at The Dell, his record with the England Under-21 side was sensational as he scored 13 goals in 11 games, earning a call up to the full England side for the game against France in February 1992. He represented England in the European Championship Finals in Sweden and then, on his arrival home, signed for Blackburn Rovers for £3.6 million. Many felt the British record fee paid for the striker a little excessive but by Boxing Day 1992, Shearer proved it was a bargain, scoring 22 goals in 25 games.

Unfortunately he was injured against Leeds and first needed a cartilage operation and then one to remove ligaments. After missing the start of the 1993-94 season, he scored 34 League and Cup goals and was by now the best striker in the country bar none. On the opening day of the 1994-95 season, he missed a penalty against his former club but it did not matter as he scored 37 League and Cup goals to be the country's top scorer and help Rovers win the Premier League title. In 1995-96 he repeated the feat, again scoring 37 goals. In doing so, he became the first player to reach 100 Premier League goals and also set a new record with five hat-tricks.

He had scored 128 goals in 162 League and Cup games for Rovers when in July 1996, the England striker, who had a superb Euro '96 tournament, joined Newcastle United for a world record £15 million. Despite being hindered by injury he duly lived up to expectations and was the Premier League's leading scorer. Despite missing half the 1997-98 season through injury, he recovered to play for England in the World Cup in France. Having had his best season for the Magpies in 1999-2000, Shearer made his international swansong as captain of England in the European Championships in 2000.

TIM SHERWOOD

Tim Sherwood began his league career with Watford, making his debut as a substitute against Sheffield Wednesday in September 1987. He had appeared in 32 league games for the Vicarage Road club when First Division Norwich City signed him for £175,000 in July 1989. He soon won a place in the Canaries' first team, playing in a variety of positions, and it wasn't long before he won selection for the England Under-21 squad. Following Andy Townsend's departure, Sherwood played in all but the last game of the 1990-91 season, but just when his career seemed set to take off, he was fined and suspended for a breach of club discipline.

Sherwood left Carrow Road in February 1992 after playing in 88 first team games and joined Blackburn Rovers for a fee of £500,000.

Though he didn't enjoy the best of form following his move, he gradually won over the Ewood crowd with his determination and drive and was appointed club captain. After leading Rovers to the Premier League title in 1994-95, he was called up to the full England squad and was elected to the PFA Premier League team as well as being on the short list for the 'Player of the Year' award. A player who always gives of his best, Sherwood went on to score 31 goals in 288 League and Cup games before being transferred to Tottenham Hotspur for £3.8 million in February 1999.

Finding White Hart Lane the ideal platform on which to rebuild his reputation as one of the best midfielders in England, he is now established as a firm favourite at the club and as possibly a key figure in England's future plans.

on New Year's Day won their only away game of the season, 2-0 at Everton. However, Rovers failed to build on their winter form and by the time spring arrived, were looking anxiously over their shoulders after a run of just one win in eight games. A 4-1 home win over Sheffield Wednesday eased their worries and safety was finally achieved with a goalless draw against Middlesbrough in the penultimate game of the season. Throughout the turmoil, suffered both on and off the pitch, one man held things together - Tony Parkes. Rovers finally got the man they wanted when former Swiss manager and then Internazionale coach Roy Hodgson was appointed in July 1997.

The new manager was very active in the transfer market, with six players being sold for a combined fee of £3.65 million, and two days either side of the start of the season a further £10 million came from the sales of Graeme Le Saux and Henning Berg to Chelsea and Manchester United respectively. Blackburn spent £6.7 million on Anders Andersson, Martin Dahlin, John Filan and Stephane Henchoz.

The new-look Rovers made a flying start to the 1997-98 campaign with 13 points from the opening five games. Aston Villa were beaten 4-0 at Villa Park, with Chris Sutton netting a hat-trick, whilst Sheffield Wednesday were demolished 7-2 at Ewood Park. In fact, Rovers' only defeat in the first 15 Premiership matches was another goal feast as Leeds United won 4-3 at Ewood Park. After this, Rovers began to find goals hard to come by and only found the net five times in the next seven games. After beating Everton 3-2 and Chelsea 1-0, Rovers seemed the main threat to Manchester United's title challenge but their visit to Old Trafford on 29 November 1997 ended in a 4-0 defeat! Rovers bounced back to be unbeaten throughout December and early in the New Year beat Aston Villa 5-0 with Kevin Gallacher scoring a hat-trick. There followed a run of four successive games when three or more goals were conceded but in one of these, Sutton netted his second hat-trick of the season as Leicester City were beaten 5-3. Two wins out of the final three games of the season ensured Rovers finished in sixth place and so qualified for their third appearance in European football the following season.

Looking to rebuild for 1998-99, Roy Hodgson broke the Blackburn bank to bring Kevin Davies to Ewood Park, paying Southampton £7.5 million for his services.

The Blue and Whites

After just two wins in the opening 15 league games, it was quite clear that Hodgson, who had spent £4.25 on Nathan Blake to bolster the attack, was living on borrowed time. Hodgson was relieved of his duties in November 1998 with Brian Kidd coming in for his first managerial task after eight years as Alex Ferguson's assistant. Under Kidd, Rovers enjoyed a mini-revival starting with a 1-0 win over Charlton Athletic when Kevin Davies scored his first goal for the club, the result ending a seven-match winless run. A further home win was recorded over Leeds United and the double completed over Villa as Rovers embarked on a run of just one defeat in ten Premiership matches. Sheffield Wednesday brought the run to an end with a crushing 4-1 victory at Ewood Park and four days later, Newcastle United won a fifth round FA Cup replay at Ewood to avenge a penalty shoot-out defeat in the League Cup. Rovers reached the quarter-final of the League Cup before losing 1-0 to Leicester City but went out in the first round of the UEFA Cup, losing 3-2 on aggregate to Olympique Lyonnais to compound their early season problems in the League. Just one of Rovers' final 14 league games ended in victory and a goalless draw at home to Manchester United in the penultimate game of the season meant that the Ewood club became the first Premier League Championship-winning side to suffer the indignity of relegation!

Kidd was a big player in the transfer market with Ashley Ward, Keith Gillespie, Jason McAteer, Matt Jansen and Lee Carsley all joining the club for a combined fee of £18 million, whilst Tim Sherwood joined Spurs for £3.8 million.

Following their relegation, Rovers were odds on to make a quick return to the Premier League, despite the departures of Chris Sutton to Chelsea, Tim Flowers to Leicester City and Stephane Henchoz to Liverpool. Brian Kidd made three summer signings, bringing in Alan Kelly, Simon Grayson and Craig Short followed by Southampton's Egil Ostenstad and Bolton's Per Frandsen. Rovers took far too long to get used to the different demands of the First Division. After a goalless home draw against Port Vale, Rovers suffered two defeats before gaining their first win over Norwich City. This was followed by a 2-0 win over Tranmere Rovers but Rovers' performances were not convincing and with an improvement in results not forthcoming, Brian Kidd was sacked at the end of October.

Tony Parkes was again given the job of caretaker-manager at Ewood

TIM FLOWERS

Tim Flowers began his league career with Wolverhampton Wanderers, making his debut at home to Sheffield United in August 1984. Although he conceded two goals in a 2-2 draw, he showed great potential and went on to play in 38 league games that season. However, the club were relegated to the Third Division and in 1985-86 were relegated yet again, this time to the Fourth Division.

Flowers had a spell on loan at Southampton without playing a match before signing for the Saints as Peter Shilton's understudy. Eventually he broke into the Southampton side on a regular basis and, after missing just five games between 1989-90 and 1991-92, was ever-present in 1992-93 when he consistently presented a formidable barrier in the club's first season in the Premier League. He kept 12 clean sheets that season, at the end of which he won his first England cap in a 1-1 draw against Brazil.

He had played in 234 games for the the Saints when in November 1993 he was allowed to join Blackburn Rovers for £2.4 million.

He showed supreme temperament when spending long spells under-employed during Rovers' Premier League Championship-winning season of 1994-95, at the end of which he was one of six Blackburn players elected to the PFA Premier League 'Team of the Year'.

At his best, Flowers was a positive influence on the team and a good shot-stopper who could inspire others, but, after a series of injuries, including a torn bicep, cost him his place in the Rovers' side, Flowers, who had appeared in 203 League and Cup games for the Ewood club, left to play for Leicester City.

Park and for his first game in charge, made eight changes to the squad as Rovers drew 2-2 with Ipswich Town. Suddenly, Rovers began to win and after home victories over Fulham (2-0), Stockport County (2-0), Bolton Wanderers (3-1) and Nottingham Forest (2-1) the club were on the verge of the play-offs. However, after Jason Wilcox had been allowed to join Leeds United, results began to fall away and Graeme Souness was appointed manager. Despite not giving up on the play-offs, Rovers ran out of games and late in the season, Charlton Athletic and Manchester City won at Ewood Park to leave the club in eleventh place.

With Preston North End and Burnley joining Rovers in the First Division for the 2000-01 season, Graeme Souness will be doing his utmost to resurrect the Blue and Whites and lead them back into the Premier League but there is a long road ahead first!

APPENDIX

Football League career statistics of every Blackburn Rovers player
since 1945

KEY:

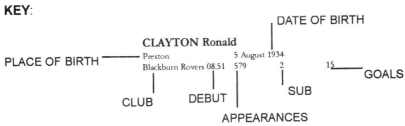

AGNEW Stephen M.

Shipley	9 November 1965		
Barnsley 11.83	186	8	29
Blackburn Rovers 06.91	2	0	0
Portsmouth(L) 11.92	3	2	0
Leicester City 02.93	52	4	4
Sunderland 01.95	56	7	9
York City 07.98	19	1	2

AINSCOW Alan

Bolton	15 July 1953		
Blackpool 07.71	178	14	28
Birmingham City 07.78	104	4	16
Everton 08.81	24	4	3
Barnsley(L) 11.82	2	0	0
Wolverhampton W 08.84	56	2	5
Blackburn Rovers 12.85	42	23	5
Rochdale 07.89	19	1	0

AIREY Jack

Bedford	28 November 1937		
Blackburn Roers 01.59	3	0	1

ALCOCK Terence

Hanley	9 December 1946		
Port Vale 09.64	112	0	0
Blackpool 08.67	190	6	21
Bury(L) 02.72	6	0	1
Blackburn Rov.(L) 12.76	3	0	1
PortVale 02.77	4	0	0
HalifaxTown 09.77	14	0	2

ANDERSON Benjamin C.

Aberdeen	18 February 1946		
Blackburn Rovers 03.64	21	7	7
Bury 07.68	51	2	4
Crystal Palace 11.73	11	0	1

ANDERSON Christopher S.

EastWemyss	28 November 1928		
Blackburn Rovers 08.50	13	0	1
Stockport County 06.53	34	0	0
Southport 07.54	28	0	0

ANDERSSON Anders P.

Tomelia,Sweden	15 March 1974		
Blackburn Rovers 07.97	1	3	0

ANDERSSON Patrik J.

Sweden	18 August 1971		
Blackburn Rovers 12.92	7	5	0

APPLEBY James P.

Shotton	15 June 1934		
Burnley 02.53	1	0	0
Blackburn Rovers 02.58	2	0	0
Southport 10.61	13	0	0
Chester City 06.62	1	0	0

ARCHIBALD Steven

Glasgow	27 September 1956		
Tottenham Hotspur 05.80	128	3	58
Blackburn Rovers 12.87	20	0	6
Reading(NC) 01.92	1	0	0

97

The Blue and Whites

| Fulham(NC) 09.92 | 2 | 0 | 0 |

ARDILLES Osvaldo C.

Argentina	3 August 1952		
Tottenham Hotspur 07.78	221	16	16
Blackburn Rov.(L) 03.88	5	0	0
QPR 08.88	4	4	0
Swindon T.(NC) 07.89	2	0	0

ARENTOFT Preben

Denmark	1 November 1942		
Newcastle United 03.69	46	4	2
Blackburn Rovers 09.71	94	0	3

ARNOLD James A.

Stafford	6 August 1950		
Blackburn Rovers 06.79	58	0	0
Everton 08.81	48	0	0
PNE(L) 10.82	6	0	0
Port Vale 08.85	53	0	0

ARNOTT Kevin W.

Gateshead	28 September 1958		
Sunderland 09.76	132	1	16
Blackburn Rov.(L) 11.81	17	0	2
Sheffield United 06.82	120	1	11
Blackburn Rov.(L) 11.82	11	1	1
RotherhamUtd (.L) 03.83	9	0	2
Chesterfield 11.87	67	4	4

ASTON John

Manchester	28 June 1947		
Manchester United 06.63	139	16	25
Luton Town 07.72	171	3	31
Mansfield Town 09.77	24	7	4
Blackburn Rovers 07.78	12	3	2

ATHERTON Dewi L.

Bangor	6 July 1951		
Blackburn Rovers 07.68	9	1	0

ATKINS Mark N.

Doncaster	14 August 1968		
Scunthorpe United 07.86	45	5	2
Blackburn Rovers 06.88	224	33	35
Wolverhampton W. 09.95	115	11	8

BAAH Peter H.

Littleborough	1 May 1973		
Blackburn Rovers 06.91	1	0	0
Fulham 07.92	38	11	4

BAILEY John A.

Liverpool	1 April 1957		
Blackburn Rovers 04.75	115	5	1
Everton 07.79	171	0	3
Newcastle United 10.85	39	1	0
Bristol City 09.88	79	1	1

BALDWIN James

Blackburn	12 January 1922		
Blackburn Rovers 12.45	88	0	0
Leicester City 02.50	180	0	4

BARKER Simon

Farnworth	4 November 1964		
Blackburn Rovers 11.82	180	2	35
QPR 07.88	291	24	33
Port Vale 09.98	23	4	2

BARTON David

Bishop Auckland	9 May 1959		
Newcastle United 05.77	101	1	5
Blackburn Rov.(L) 08.82	8	0	1
Darlington 02.83	49	0	3

BARTON John B.

Wigan	27 April 1942		
Preston North End 05.59	48	0	0
Blackburn Rovers 06.66	68	0	0

BATTY David

Leeds	2 December 1968		
Leeds United 08.87	201	10	4
Blackburn Rovers 10.93	53	1	1
Newcastle United 03.96	81	2	3
Leeds United 12.98	10	0	0

BEAMISH Kenneth G.

Bebington	25 August 1947		
Tranmere Rovers 07.66	176	1	49
Brighton & HA 03.72	86	10	27
Blackburn Rovers 05.74	86	0	19
Port Vale 09.76	84	1	29
Bury 09.78	49	0	20
Tranmere Rovers 11.79	57	2	15
Swindon Town 08.81	1	1	0

BEAN Alan

Doncaster	17 January 1935		
Blackburn Rovers 04.52	2	0	0

BEARDALL James T.

Whitefield	18 October 1946		
Blackburn Rovers 03.68	4	2	1
Oldham Athletic 05.69	21	1	10

BEARDSMORE Russell P.

Wigan	28 September 1968		
Manchester United 09.86	30	26	4
Blackburn Rovers 12.91	1	1	0
Bournemouth 06.93	167	11	4

BEATTIE James S.

Lancaster	27February1978		
Blackburn Rovers 03.95	1	3	0
Southampton 07.98	30	23	5

BECKFORD Jason N.

Manchester	14 February 1970		
Manchester City 08.87	8	12	1
Blackburn Rov.(L) 03.91	3	1	0
Port Vale(L) 09.91	4	1	1
Birmingham City 01.92	5	2	2
Bury(L) 03.94	3	0	0
Stoke City 08.94	2	2	0
Millwall 12.94	6	3	0
Northampton T. 05.95	0	1	0

BEE Francis E.

Nottingham	23 January 1927		
Sunderland 06.47	5	0	1
Blackburn Rovers 03.49	4	0	0

BEGLIN James M.

Waterford	29 July 1963		
Liverpool 05.83	64	0	2
Leeds United 07.89	18	1	0
Plymouth A.(L) 11.89	5	0	0
Blackburn Rov.(L) 10.90	6	0	0

BELL Eric J.

Bedlington	13 February 1922		
Blackburn Rovers 05.45	323	0	9

BELL Norman

Hylton Castle	16 November 1955		
Wolverhampton W. 11.73	58	22	17
Blackburn Rovers 11.81	57	4	10

BELL Robert C.

Cambridge	26 October 1950		
Ipswich Town 10.68	32	0	1
Blackburn Rovers 09.71	2	0	0
Crystal Palace 09.71	31	0	0
Norwich City 02.72	3	0	0
York City 02.77	5	0	0

BERG Henning

Norway	1 September 1969		
Blackburn Rovers 01.93	154	5	4
Manchester United 08.97	33	10	1

BIMPSON Louis J.

Rainford	14 May 1929		
Liverpool 01.53	94	0	39
Blackburn Rovers 11.59	22	0	5
Bournemouth 02.61	11	0	1
Rochdale 08.61	54	0	16

BINNS Eric

Halifax	13 August 1924		
Halifax Town 05.46	6	0	1
Burnley 03.49	15	0	0
Blackburn Rovers 05.55	23	0	0

BIRCHENALL Alan J.

EastHam	22 August 1945		
Sheffield United 06.63	106	1	31
Chelsea 11.67	74	1	20
Crysta lPalace 06.70	41	0	11
Leicester City 09.71	156	7	12
Notts County(L) 03.76	5	0	0
Notts County 09.77	28	0	0
Blackburn Rovers 07.78	17	1	0
Luton Town 03.79	9	1	0
Hereford United 10.79	11	0	0

BLACKLAW Adam S.

Aberdeen	2 September 1937		
Burnley 10.54	318	0	0
Blackburn Rovers 07.67	96	0	0
Blackpool 06.70	1	0	0

BLAKE Nathan A.

Cardiff	27 January 1972		
Cardiff City 03.90	113	18	35
Sheffield United 02.94	55	14	34
Bolton Wanderers 12.95	102	5	38
Blackburn Rovers 10.98	26	13	6

BLORE Reginald

Wrexham	18 March 1942		
Liverpool 05.59	1	0	0
Southport 07.60	139	0	55
BlackburnRovers 11.63	11	0	0
Oldham Athletic 12.65	182	5	20

BOGAN Thomas

Glasgow	18 May 1920		
Preston North End 10.48	11	0	0
Manchester United 08.49	29	0	7
Southampton 02.51	8	0	2

Blackburn Rovers 08.53   1   0   0

BRADFORD David W.

Manchester	22 February 1953		
Blackburn Rovers 08.71	58	6	3
Sheffield United 07.74	54	6	3
Peterborough U.(L) 10.76	4	0	0
Coventry City 10.81	6	0	1

BRADSHAW Alan

Blackburn	14 September 1941		
Blackburn Rovers 7.63	11	0	2
Crewe Alexandra 05.65	287	7	50

BRADSHAW Paul W.

Altrincham	28 April 1956		
Blackburn Rovers 07.73	78	0	0
Wolverhampton W. 09.77	200	0	0
WBA 04.85	8	0	0
Bristol Rov.(NC) 03.87	5	0	0
Newport Co.(NC) 07.87	23	0	0
WBA 08.88	6	0	0
Peterborough Utd. 06.90	39	0	0

BRANAGAN James P.S.

Urmston	3 July 1955		
Oldham Athletic 07.73	24	3	0
Huddersfield Town 11.77	37	1	0
Blackburn Rovers 10.79	290	4	5
Preston North End 05.87	3	0	0
York City 10.87	40	2	1

BRAY John

Rishton	16 March 1937		
Blackburn Rovers 03.54	153	0	2
Bury 04.65	32	0	0

BRIGGS Thomas H.

Chesterfield	27 November 1923		
Grimsby Town 05.47	116	0	78
Coventry City 01.51	11	0	7
Birmingham City 09.51	50	0	22
Blackburn Rov. 12.52	194	0	140
Grimsby Town 03.58	19	0	9

BRITT Martin C.

Leigh-on-Sea	17 January 1948		
West Ham United 01.63	20	0	6
Blackburn Rovers 03.66	8	0	0

BROOMES Marlon C.

Birmingham	28 November 1977		
Blackburn Rovers 11.94	23	7	1
Swindon Town(L) 01.97	12	0	1

BROTHERSTON Noel

Dundonald	18 November 1956		
Tottenham H. 04.74	1	0	0
Blackburn Rovers 07.77	307	10	40
Bury 06.87	32	6	4
Scarborough(L) 10.88	5	0	0

BROWN Keith

Edinburgh	24 December 1979		
Blackburn Rovers 04.99	0	2	0

BROWN Richard A.

Nottingham	13 January 1967		
Blackburn Rovers 09.90	26	2	0
Maidstone Utd.(L) 02.91	3	0	0
Stockport County 03.95	1	0	0
Blackpool 08.95	2	1	0

BURGESS Benjamin

Buxton	9 November 1981		
Blackburn Rovers 04.99	1	1	0

BURGIN Andrew

Sheffield	6 March 1947		
Sheffield Wed. 03.64	1	0	0
Rotherham United 08.67	9	1	0
Halifax Town 12.68	243	0	9
Blackburn Rovers 09.74	45	0	1

BURKE Marshall

Glasgow	26 March 1959		
Burnley 03.77	22	2	5
Leeds United 05.80	0	0	0
Blackburn Rovers 12.80	34	5	7
Lincoln City 10.82	49	1	7
Cardiff City(L) 12.83	3	0	0
Tranmere Rovers 09.84	3	0	0

BUSBY Vivian D.

High Wycombe	19 June 1949		
Luton Town 01.70	64	13	16
Newcastle United 12.71	4	0	2
Fulham 08.73	114	4	29
Norwich City 09.76	22	0	11
Stoke City 11.77	33	17	9
Sheffield Utd.(L) 01.80	3	0	1
Blackburn Rovers 02.81	8	0	1
York City(NC) 08.82	9	10	4

BUTCHER John M.

Newcastle	27 May 1956		
Blackburn Rovers 03.76	104	0	0
Oxford United 07.82	16	0	0
Halifax Town(L) 09.82	5	0	0

Bury(L) 12.83	11	0	0
Chester City 08.84	84	0	0
Bury(L) 10.85	5	0	0

BUTT Leonard

Wilmslow	26 August 1910		
Stockport County 08.28	8	0	1
Huddersfield Town 05.35	67	0	11
Blackburn Rovers 01.37	110	0	44
YorkCity 01.47	25	0	2
Mansfield Town 10.47	15	0	4

BYRNE David S.

Hammersmith	5 March 1961		
Gillingham 07.85	18	5	3
Millwall 07.86	52	11	6
Cambridge Utd.(L) 09.88	4	0	0
Blackburn Rov.(L) 02.89	4	0	0
Plymouth Argyle 03.89	52	7	2
Bristol Rovers(L) 02.90	0	2	0
Watford 11.90	16	1	2
Reading(L) 08.91	7	0	2
Fulham(L) 01.92	5	0	0
Walsall(L) 02.94	5	0	0

BYROM John

Blackburn	28 July 1944		
Blackburn Rovers 08.61	106	2	45
Bolton Wanderers 06.66	296	8	113
Blackburn Rovers 09.76	15	1	5

CAIRNS Ronald

Chopwell	4 April 1934		
Blackburn Rovers 09.53	26	0	7
Rochdale 06.59	195	0	66
Southport 07.64	34	0	13

CALLOWAY Laurence J.

Birmingham	17 June 1945		
Rochdale 07.64	161	1	4
Blackburn Rovers 03.68	17	8	1
Southport 08.70	45	0	7
York City 06.71	54	1	3
Shrewsbury Town 12.72	77	5	3

CAMPBELL John

Liverpool	17 March 1922		
Blackburn Rovers 12.45	224	0	19
Oldham Athletic 07.56	26	0	5

CARSLEY Lee K.

Birmingham	28 February 1974		
Derby County 07.92	122	16	5
Blackburn Rovers 03.99	40	1	10

CARTER Donald F.

Midsomer Norton	11 September 1921		
Bury 01.39	56	0	27
Blackburn Rovers 06.48	2	0	0
New Brighton1 1.48	105	0	19

CHADWICK Frank R.

Blackburn	9 November 1927		
Blackburn Rovers06.46	11	0	1

CHAPPELL Leslie A.

Nottingham	6 February 1947		
Rotherham United 02.65	106	2	37
Blackburn Rovers 05.68	7	0	0
Reading 07.69	193	8	78
Doncaster Rovers 12.74	57	1	10
Swansea City 07.76	65	2	5

CHARTER Raymond

Ashton-under-Lyne	10 January 1950		
Blackburn Rovers 01.68	13	5	0
Stockport County 07.71	87	4	2

CLAYTON Kenneth

Preston	6 April 1933		
Blackburn Rovers 05.50	72	0	0

CLAYTON Ronald

Preston	5 August 1934		
Blackburn Rovers 08.51	579	2	15

CLINTON Thomas J.

Dublin	13 April 1926		
Everton 03.48	73	0	4
Blackburn Rovers 04.55	6	0	0
Tranmere Rovers 06.56	9	0	0

CODDINGTON John W.

Worksop	16 December 1937		
Huddersfield Town 01.55	332	0	17
Blackburn Rovers 06.67	72	1	3
Stockport County 01.70	52	0	0

COLEMAN Christopher

Swansea	10 June 1970		
Swansea City 08.87	159	1	2
Crystal Palace 07.91	143	11	13
Blackburn Rovers 12.95	27	1	0
Fulham 12.97	111	0	8

COLLIER Darren J.

Stockton	1 December 1967		
Blackburn Rovers 12.87	27	0	0
Darlington 07.93	44	0	0

COMSTIVE Paul T.

Southport	25 November 1961		
Blackburn Rovers 10.79	3	3	0
Rochdale(L) 09.82	9	0	2
Wigan Athletic 08.83	35	0	2
Wrexham 11.84	95	4	8
Burnley 07.87	81	1	17
Bolton Wanderers 09.89	42	7	3
Chester City 11.91	55	2	6

CONLON Bryan

Shildon	14 January 1943		
Darlington 08.64	71	3	27
Millwall 11.67	40	1	13
Norwich City 12.68	29	0	8
Blackburn Rovers 05.70	43	2	7
Crewe Alex.(L) 01.72	4	0	1
Cambridge United 03.72	17	1	3
Hartlepool United 09.72	38	3	3

CONNELLY John M.

StHelens	18 July 1938		
Burnley 11.56	215	0	86
Manchester United 04.64	79	1	22
Blackburn Rovers 09.66	148	1	36
Bury 06.70	128	0	37

COOK Leslie

Blackburn	11 November 1924		
Blackburn Rovers 11.41	76	0	0
Coventry City 07.49	88	0	0

COUGHLIN Russell J.

Swansea	15 February 1960		
Blackburn Rovers 03.79	22	2	0
Carlisle United 10.80	114	16	13
Plymouth Argyle 07.84	128	3	18
Blackpool 12.87	100	2	8
Shrewsbury T.(L)09.90	4	1	0
Swansea City 10.90	99	2	2
Exeter City 07.93	64	4	0
Torquay United 10.95	2	3	0

COXON Gary E.

Liverpool	31 May 1946		
Blackburn Rovers 12.63	10	0	0

CRAIG Joseph

Logie	14 May 1954		
Blackburn Rovers 09.78	44	4	8

CRAIG Robert M.

Airdrie	8 April 1935		
Sheffield Wed. 11.59	84	0	25

Blackburn Rovers 04.62	8	0	3
Oldham Athletic 03.64	18	0	4

CRAWFORD Andrew

Filey	30 January 1959		
Derby County 01.77	16	5	4
Blackburn Rovers 10.79	56	0	21
Bournemouth 11.81	31	2	10
Cardiff City 08.83	6	0	1
Middlesbrough 10.83	8	1	1
Stockport Co.(NC) 12.84	6	0	2
Torquay Utd.(NC) 02.85	3	0	0

CROFT Gary

Burton-on-Trent	17 February 1974		
Grimsby Town 07.92	139	10	3
Blackburn Rovers 03.96	33	7	1

CROMPTON Alan

Bolton	6 March 1958		
Blackburn Rovers 07.76	2	2	0
Wigan Athletic 07.78	7	7	0

CROOK Walter

Chorley	28 April 1913		
Blackburn Rovers 01.31	218	0	2
Bolton Wanderers 05.47	28	0	0

CROSSAN Edward

Derry (N.Ireland)	17 November 1925		
Blackburn Rovers 11.47	287	0	73
Tranmere Rovers 08.57	39	0	6

CROWE Christopher

Newcastle	11 June 1939		
Leeds United 06.56	95	0	27
Blackburn Rovers 03.60	51	0	6
Wolverhampton W. 02.62	83	0	24
Nottingham Forest 08.64	73	0	12
Bristol City 01.67	66	1	13
Walsall 09.69	10	3	1

CURRY Sean P.

Liverpool	13 November 1966		
Blackburn Rovers 01.87	25	13	6
Hartlepool United 08.89	0	1	0

CURTIS John

Poulton-le-Fylde	2 September 1954		
Blackpool 09.72	96	6	0
Blackburn Rovers 07.77	9	1	0
Wigan Athletic 03.79	32	0	0

DAHLIN Martin

Udevalla, Sweden	16 April 1968		
Blackburn Rovers 07.97	13	13	4

DAILLY Christian E.

Dundee	23 October 1973		
Derby County 08.96	62	5	4
Blackburn Rovers 08.98	58	3	4

DALY Patrick J.

Manchester	3 January 1941		
Blackburn Rovers 01.58	3	0	0
Southport 02.62	10	0	0

DARLING Malcolm

Arbroath	4 July 1947		
Blackburn Rovers 10.64	114	14	30
Norwich City 05.70	16	0	5
Rochdale 10.71	82	4	16
Bolton Wanderers 09.73	6	2	0
Chesterfield 08.74	100	4	33
Stockport Co.(L) 03.77	1	0	2
Sheffield Wed. 08.77	1	1	0
Hartlepool United 09.77	2	2	0
Bury(NC) 03.78	1	1	0

DAVIDSON Callum I.

Stirling	25 June 1976		
Blackburn Rovers 02.98	62	2	1

DAVIES Kevin C.

Sheffield	26 March 1977		
Chesterfield 04.94	113	16	22
Southampton 05.97	20	5	9
Blackburn Rovers 06.98	11	12	1

DAWSON Alistair J.

Govan	25 February 1958		
Blackburn Rovers 08.87	32	8	0

DEVINE Peter

Blackburn	25 May 1960		
Bristol City 07.81	19	2	1
Blackburn R.(NC) 09.82	8	0	2
Burnley 06.84	46	10	4

DEVRIES Roger

Hull	25October1950		
Hull City 09.67	314	4	0
Blackburn Rovers 07.80	13	0	0
Scunthorpe United 10.81	6	0	1

DIAMOND Anthony J.

Rochdale	23 August 1968		
Blackburn Rovers 06.86	9	17	3
Wigan Athletic(L) 10.88	6	0	2
Blackpool 08.89	2	1	1

DICKINS Matthew J.

Sheffield	3 September 1970		
Lincoln City 02.91	27	0	0
Blackburn Rovers 03.92	1	0	0
Blackpool(L) 01.93	19	0	0
Rochdale(L) 10.94	4	0	0
Stockport County 02.95	12	1	0

DOBING Peter A.

Manchester	1 December 1938		
Blackburn Rovers 12.55	179	0	88
Manchester City 07.61	82	0	31
Stoke City 08.63	303	4	82

DOBSON Anthony J.

Coventry	5 February 1969		
Coventry City 07.86	51	3	1
Blackburn Rovers 01.91	36	5	0
Portsmouth 09.93	48	5	2
Oxford United(L) 12.94	5	0	0
Peterborough U.(L) 01.96	4	0	0
WBA 08.97	6	5	0
Gillingham(L) 09.98	2	0	0
Northampton T. 09.98	8	3	0

DONIS Georgios

Greece	22 October 1969		
Blackburn Rovers 07.96	11	11	2
Sheffield United 03.99	5	2	1

DONNELLY Darren C.

Liverpool	28 December 1971		
Blackburn Rovers 06.90	1	1	0
Chester City 08.93	0	9	0

DOUGAN Derek A.

Belfast	20 January 1938		
Portsmouth 08.57	33	0	9
Blackburn Rovers 03.59	59	0	26
Aston Villa 08.61	51	0	19
Peterborough Utd. 06.63	77	0	38
Leicester City 05.65	68	0	35
Wolverhampton W .03.67	244	14	95

DOUGLAS Bryan

Blackburn	27 May 1934		
Blackburn Rovers 04.52	438	0	100

The Blue and Whites

DOWNES Steven F.

Leeds	2 December 1949		
Rotherham United 04.67	54	5	18
Sheffield Wed. 12.69	26	4	4
Chesterfield 08.72	37	4	11
Halifax Town 07.74	38	12	12
Blackburn Rov.(L) 03.76	6	0	0

DUFF Damien A.

Ballyboden,Ireland	2 March 1979		
Blackburn Rovers 03.96	68	25	10

DUNN David

Blackburn	27 December 1979		
Blackburn Rovers 09.97	27	8	4

DUNNING William S.

Bury	15 November 1952		
Blackburn Rovers 11.70	10	3	2

DUXBURY Michael

Blackburn	1 September 1959		
Manchester United 10.76	274	25	6
Blackburn Rovers 08.90	25	2	0
Bradford City 01.92	64	1	0

ECCLES Terence S.

Leeds	2 March 1952		
Blackburn Rovers 08.69	33	13	6
Mansfield Town 07.73	115	3	47
Huddersfield Town 01.77	41	5	6
York City 09.79	64	0	18

ECKERSLEY William

Southport	16 July 1925		
Blackburn Rovers 03.48	406	0	20

EDDS Ernest F.

Portsmouth	19 March 1926		
Plymouth Argyle 10.46	59	0	18
Blackburn Rovers 12.49	18	0	3
Torquay United 06.51	84	0	34
Plymouth Argyle 10.53	26	0	4
Swindon Town 07.55	3	0	0

ELSE Frederick

Golborne	31 March 1933		
Preston North End 08.53	215	0	0
Blackburn Rovers 08.61	187	0	0
Barrow 07.66	148	0	0

ELVY Reginald

Leeds	25 November 1920		
Halifax Town 03.44	22	0	0

Bolton Wanderers 03.47	31	0	0
Blackburn Rovers 11.51	192	0	0
Northampton T. 07.56	67	0	0

ENDEAN Barry

Chester-le-Street	22 March 1946		
Watford 09.68	72	5	28
Charlton Athletic 02.71	27	0	1
Blackburn Rovers 10.71	65	14	18
Huddersfield Town 03.75	8	4	1
Workington(L) 10.75	8	0	2
Hartlepool United 03.76	24	1	5

ENGLAND Michael H.

Holywell	2 December 1941		
Blackburn Rovers 04.59	165	0	21
Tottenham Hotspur 08.66	300	0	14
Cardiff City 08.75	40	0	1

FARRELL Gerard W.

Liverpool	19 March 1952		
Blackburn Rovers 10.71	21	1	1

FAZACKERLEY Derek W.

Preston	5 November 1951		
Blackburn Rovers 10.69	593	3	23
ChesterCity 01.87	66	0	0
York City 07.88	16	0	0
Bury 12.88	7	7	0

FEAR Keith W.

Bristol	8 May 1952		
Bristol City 06.69	126	25	32
Hereford United(L) 09.77	6	0	0
Blackburn Rov.(L) 12.77	5	0	2
Plymouth Argyle 02.78	40	5	9
Brentford(L) 11.79	7	1	2
Chester City 01.80	41	3	3

FENTON Graham A.

Wallsend	22 May 1974		
Aston Villa 02.92	16	16	3
WBA(L) 01.94	7	0	3
Blackburn Rovers 11.95	9	18	7
Leicester City 08.97	12	20	3

FENTON William H.

Hartlepool	23 June 1926		
Blackburn Rovers 12.48	33	0	7
York City 05.51	258	0	118

FERGUSON Michael K.

Burnley	9 March 1943		
Accrington Stanley 07.60	23	0	1
Blackburn Rovers 03.62	220	0	29

Aston Villa 05.68	38	0	2
QPR 11.69	67	1	2
Cambridge United 07.73	39	0	4
Rochdale 07.74	68	1	5
Halifax Town 12.76	2	0	0

FETTIS Alan W.

Belfast	1 February 1971		
Hull City 08.91	131	4	2
WBA(L) 11.95	3	0	0
Nottingham Forest 01.96	4	0	0
Blackburn Rovers 09.97	9	2	0

FIELD Anthony

Halifax	6 July 1946		
Halifax Town 07.63	21	0	3
Barrow 08.66	36	2	16
Southport 03.68	127	6	41
Blackburn Rovers 10.71	104	2	45
Sheffield United 03.74	63	3	13

FILAN John R.

Sydney, Australia	8 February 1970		
Cambridge United 03.93	68	0	0
Coventry City 03.95	15	1	0
Blackburn Rovers 07.97	49	0	0

FINNIGAN Anthony

Wimbledon	17 October 1962		
Crystal Palace 02.85	94	11	10
Blackburn Rovers 07.88	21	15	0
HullCity 07.90	15	3	1
Swindon Town 03.91	2	1	0
Brentford(NC) 01.92	3	0	0
Barnet(NC) 09.93	5	1	1
Fulham(NC) 09.94	8	5	0

FLITCROFT Garry W.

Bolton	6 November 1972		
Manchester City 07.91	109	6	13
Bury(L)03.92	12	0	0
Blackburn Rovers 03.96	83	7	5

FLOWERS Timothy D.

Kenilworth	3 February 1967		
Wolverhampton W. 08.84	63	0	0
Southampton 06.86	192	0	0
Swindon Town(L) 03.87	2	0	0
Swindon Town(L) 11.87	5	0	0
Blackburn Rovers 11.93	175	2	0
Leicester City08.99	32	0	0

FOWLER Martin

York	17 January 1957		
Huddersfield Town 01.74	62	11	2

Blackburn Rovers 07.78	36	2	0
Hartlepool Utd.(L) 03.80	6	0	0

FRANDSEN Per

Copenhagen	6 February 1970		
Bolton Wanderers 08.96	129	1	16
Blackburn Rovers 09.99	25	4	5

FRYATT James E.

Southampton	2 September 1940		
Charlton Athletic 10.57	5	0	3
Southend United 06.60	61	0	24
Bradford PA 06.63	101	0	38
Southport 03.66	39	0	15
Torquay United 03.67	27	0	11
Stockport County 10.67	45	0	28
Blackburn Rovers 10.68	29	8	5
Oldham Athletic 02.70	76	0	40
Southport 11.71	102	2	24
Stockport County 09.74	1	0	1
Torquay United 12.74	3	0	0

GALE Anthony P.

Westminster	19 November 1959		
Fulham 08.77	277	0	19
West Ham United 07.84	293	7	5
Blackburn Rovers 08.94	15	0	0
Crystal Palace 09.95	2	0	0

GALLACHER Bernard

Johnstone	22 March 1967		
Aston Villa 03.85	55	2	0
Blackburn Rov.(L) 11.90	4	0	0
Doncaster Rovers 09.91	2	0	0
Brighton & HA 10.91	45	0	1
North'pton T.(NC) 01.94	5	0	0

GALLACHER Kevin W.

Clydebank	23November1966		
Coventry City 01.90	99	1	28
Blackburn Rovers03.93	132	13	46

GARBETT Terence W.

Lanchester	9 September 1945		
Middlesbrough 08.63	7	0	1
Watford 08.66	196	4	46
Blackburn Rovers 09.71	90	0	6
Sheffield United 02.74	26	5	0

GARNER Simon

Boston	23 November 1959		
Blackburn Rovers 07.78	455	29	168
WBA 08.92	25	8	8
Wycombe W. 02.94	53	13	15
Torquay United(L) 01.96	10	1	1

105

GAYLE Howard A.

Liverpool	18 May 1958		
Liverpool 11.77	3	1	1
Fulham(L) 01.80	14	0	0
Newcastle Utd.(L) 11.82	8	0	2
Birmingham City 01.83	45	1	9
Sunderland 08.84	39	9	4
Stoke City 03.87	4	2	2
Blackburn Rovers 07.87	97	19	29
Halifax Town(NC) 08.92	2	3	0

GENNOE Terence W.

Shrewsbury	16 March 1953		
Bury 06.73	3	0	0
Halifax Town 05.75	75	0	0
Southampton 02.78	36	0	0
Crystal Palace(L) 01.81	3	0	0
Blackburn Rovers 08.81	289	0	0

GILLESPIE Keith R.

Bangor	18 February 1975		
Manchester United 02.93	3	6	1
Wigan Athletic(L) 09.93	8	0	4
Newcastle United01.95	94	19	11
Blackburn Rovers 12.98	24	13	3

GILLIVER Allan H.

Swallownest	3 August 1944		
Huddersfield Town 08.61	45	0	22
Blackburn Rovers 06.66	32	2	9
Rotherham United 05.68	24	3	2
Brighton & HA 07.69	54	3	19
Lincoln City 02.71	33	4	8
Bradford City 06.72	68	2	30
Stockport County 06.74	22	3	5
Bradford City(NC) 08.78	1	1	0

GIVEN Seamus J.

Lifford	20 April 1976		
Blackburn Rovers 08.94	2	0	0
Swindon Town(L) 08.95	5	0	0
Sunderland(L) 01.96	17	0	0
NewcastleUnited07.97	55	0	0

GLAISTER George

Bywell	18 May 1918		
Blackburn Rovers 05.37	8	0	1
Stockport County 04.47	92	0	21
Halifax Town 08.50	34	0	7
Accrington Stanley 09.51	24	0	1

GLENN David A.

Wigan	30 November 1962		
Wigan Athletic 11.80	68	4	4

Blackburn Rovers 08.83	23	1	0
Chester City 07.85	70	3	1

GLOVER Alexander

Glasgow	28 February 1922		
Bradford PA 03.48	48	0	5
Luton Town 09.49	58	0	6
BlackburnRovers 09.51	65	0	4
Barrow 08.54	86	0	7

GODWIN Verdi

Blackburn	11 February 1926		
Blackburn Rovers 03.46	27	0	6
Manchester City 06.48	8	0	3
Stoke City 06.49	22	0	2
Mansfield Town 01.50	31	0	9
Grimsby Town 01.52	1	0	0
Brentford 03.52	7	0	1
Southport 07.54	17	0	2
Barrow 08.55	16	0	3
Tranmere Rovers 08.56	14	0	2

GOODWIN Frederick J.

Stockport	4 January 1944		
Wolverhampton W. 01.61	44	1	0
Stockport County 01.66	171	5	20
Blackburn Rovers 03.70	63	1	4
Southport 10.71	10	2	0
Port Vale 08.72	27	0	2
Stockport County 08.74	29	0	1

GRAHAM Leslie

Manchester	14 May 1924		
Blackburn Rovers 04.47	150	0	42
Newport County 02.53	97	0	40
Watford 07.55	90	0	26
Newport County 09.57	65	0	15

GRAY David

Cupar, Angus	8 February 1922		
PrestonNorthEnd 05.47	36	0	0
Blackburn Rovers 08.48	107	0	5

GRAYSON Simon N.

Ripon	16 December 1969		
Leeds United 06.88	2	0	0
Leicester City 03.92	175	13	4
Aston Villa 07.97	32	16	0
Blackburn Rovers 07.99	31	3	0

GREGORY David H.

Peterborough	6 October 1951		
Peterborough Utd. 08.73	125	17	32
Stoke City 06.77	22	1	3
BlackburnRovers 07.78	5	0	3

Bury 09.78	50	2	13
Portsmouth 12.79	63	10	18
Wrexham 08.82	145	8	31
Peterborough Utd. 08.86	16	15	8

GRIFFITHS Barry
| Manchester | 21 November 1933 | | |
| Blackburn Rovers 07.62 | 2 | 0 | 0 |

GUEST William F.
Birmingham	8 February 1914		
Birmingham City 02.32	76	0	15
West Ham United 03.36	3	0	1
Blackburn Rovers 01.37	88	0	30
Walsall 08.47	5	0	0

HAMILTON David
SouthShields	7 November 1960		
Blackburn Rovers 01.81	104	10	7
Cardiff City(L) 03.85	10	0	0
Wigan Athletic 07.86	97	6	7
Chester City 08.89	26	2	0
Burnley 08.90	11	4	0

HARGREAVES David
| Accrington | 27 August 1954 | | |
| Blackburn Rovers 12.77 | 2 | 0 | 0 |

HARKNESS Steven
Carlisle	27 August 1971		
Carlisle United 03.89	12	1	0
Liverpool 07.89	90	12	2
Huddersfield T.(L) 09.93	5	0	0
Southend Utd.(L) 02.95	6	0	0
Blackburn Rovers 09.99	16	1	0

HARRIS Joseph
Belfast	8 April 1929		
Blackburn Rovers 01.51	35	0	15
Oldham Athletic 03.53	27	0	4

HARRISON Michael J.
Ilford	18 April 1940		
Chelsea 04.57	61	0	8
Blackburn Rovers 09.62	160	0	40
Plymouth Argyle 09.67	15	0	3
Luton Town 06.68	28	3	6

HAVERTY Joseph
Dublin	17 February 1936		
Arsenal 07.54	114	0	25
Blackburn Rovers 08.61	27	0	1
Millwall 09.62	68	0	8
Bristol Rovers 12.64	13	0	1

HAWKINS Graham N.
Darlaston	5 March 1946		
Wolverhampton W. 06.63	28	6	0
Preston North End 01.68	241	4	3
Blackburn Rovers 06.74	108	1	4
Port Vale 01.78	61	1	3

HAYHURST Stanley H.
Leyland	13 May 1925		
Blackburn Rovers 01.43	27	0	0
Tottenham Hotspur 10.48	0	0	0
Barrow 06.50	26	0	0
Grimsby Town 01.51	62	0	0

HEATON Michael J.
Sheffield	15 January 1947		
Sheffield United 11.64	31	2	0
Blackburn Rovers 10.71	168	2	1

HELLIWELL David
Blackburn	28 March 1948		
Blackburn Rovers 05.66	15	0	1
Lincoln City 05.69	11	2	1
Workington 07.70	184	13	20
Rochdale 07.76	20	11	3

HENCHOZ Stephane
| Billens, Switzerland | 7 September 1974 | | |
| Blackburn Rovers 07.97 | 70 | 0 | 0 |

HENDREY Colin E.J.
Keith	7 December 1965		
Blackburn Rovers 03.87	99	3	22
Manchester City 11.89	57	6	5
Blackburn Rovers 11.91	229	5	12

HERRON Alan
| Ashington | 6 October 1932 | | |
| Blackburn Rovers 08.50 | 4 | 0 | 0 |

HICKMAN Michael F.T.
Elstead	2 October 1946		
Brighton & HA 06.65	12	3	0
Grimsby Town 06.68	247	7	48
Blackburn Rovers 02.75	23	3	8
Torquay United 10.75	17	0	1

HIGGINS George
Dundee	16 June 1925		
Blackburn Rovers 10.46	53	0	0
Bolton Wanderers 07.51	69	0	0
Grimsby Town 05.54	47	0	0

HILDERSLEY Ronald

Kirkcaldy	6 April 1965		
Manchester City 04.83	1	0	0
Chester City(L) 01.84	9	0	0
Chester City 07.84	5	4	0
Rochdale(NC) 08.85	12	4	0
Preston North End 06.86	54	4	3
Cambridge Utd.(L) 02.88	9	0	3
Blackburn Rovers 07.88	25	5	4
Wigan Athletic 08.90	4	0	0
Halifax Town 11.91	21	10	2

HILL Brian

Mansfield	15 December 1942		
Grimsby Town 08.60	180	0	26
Huddersfield Town 11.66	85	3	6
Blackburn Rovers 09.69	34	3	4
Torquay United 07.71	6	1	1

HILL Keith J.

Bolton	17 May 1969		
Blackburn Rovers 05.87	89	7	4
Plymouth Argyle 09.92	117	6	2
Rochdale 07.96	112	1	6

HILTON Patrick J.

Aylesham	1 May 1954		
Brighton & HA 02.73	18	2	2
Blackburn Rovers 05.74	16	0	2
Gillingham 09.75	16	10	1
Aldershot(L) 03.77	12	1	0
Southport 07.77	22	5	5

HINDSON Gordon

Stanley	8 January 1950		
Newcastle United 08.68	7	0	1
Luton Town 10.71	62	6	3
Carlisle United(L) 09.75	1	2	0
Blackburn Rovers 10.75	10	0	0

HIRD Kevin

Colne	11 February 1955		
Blackburn Rovers 02.73	129	3	20
Leeds United 03.79	165	16	19
Burnley 08.84	83	0	23

HOLDEN Alan

Haslingden	12 October 1941		
Blackburn Rovers 01.62	1	0	0
Stockport County 07.66	1	0	0

HOLE Barrington G.

Swansea	16 September 1942		
Cardiff City 09.59	211	0	16
Blackburn Rovers 07.66	79	0	13

Aston Villa 09.68	47	0	6
Swansea City 07.70	78	0	3

HOLLIDAY Kevin J.

Darwen	19 August 1925		
Blackburn Rovers 10.46	29	0	0
Accrington Stanley 07.52	96	0	5
Barrow 09.55	5	0	0

HOLMES Matthew J.

Luton	1 August 1969		
Bournemouth 08.88	105	9	8
Cardiff City(L) 03.89	0	1	0
West Ham United 08.92	63	13	4
Blackburn Rovers 08.95	8	1	1
Charlton Athletic 07.97	10	6	1

HOLMES William

Hunslet	29 October 1926		
Doncaster Rovers 10.50	2	0	0
Blackburn Rovers 01.52	21	0	16
Bradford City 09.53	22	0	5
Southport 07.54	56	0	21

HOLT David

Sunniside	7 January 1945		
Blackburn Rovers 04.63	10	0	0

HOLT William K.

Boldon	31 March 1926		
Blackburn Rovers 01.49	78	0	0
Barrow 06.54	72	0	0

HORREY Rowland G.

Bishop Auckland	7 March 1943		
Blackburn Rovers 12.63	3	0	0
York City 07.66	74	0	9
Cambridge United 07.68	37	1	4

HORTON Henry

Ledbury	18 April 1923		
Blackburn Rovers 01.47	92	0	5
Southampton 06.51	75	0	12
Bradford PA 05.54	26	0	0

HOY Robert

Halifax	10 January 1950		
Huddersfield Town 11.67	140	4	18
Blackburn Rovers 03.75	13	6	0
Halifax Town 06.76	30	0	7
York City 08.77	10	4	1
Rochdale 12.77	61	5	12

HUDSON George A.

Manchester	14 March 1937		
Blackburn Rovers 01.58	4	0	1
Accrington Stanley 07.60	44	0	35
Peterborough Utd. 10.61	65	0	39
Coventry City 04.63	113	0	62
Northampton T. 03.66	18	0	6
Tranmere Rovers 01.67	53	1	20

HUGHES William A.

Holyhead	2 February 1919		
Tottenham H.12.45	2	0	0
Blackburn Rovers 10.48	27	0	0
Rochdale 09.50	9	0	0
Crystal Palace 02.51	18	0	0

HUNTER Allan

SionMills,N.Ireland	30 June 1946		
Oldham Athletic 01.67	83	0	1
Blackburn Rovers 06.69	84	0	1
Ipswich Town 09.71	280	0	8
Colchester United 05.82	18	1	0

HUTCHINS Donald

Middlesbrough	8 May 1948		
Leicester City 02.66	4	0	0
Plymouth Argyle 07.69	94	1	23
Blackburn Rovers 07.72	37	3	6
Bradford City 06.74	252	4	44

HUTT Geoffrey

Duffield	28 September 1949		
Huddersfield Town 09.67	245	0	4
Blackburn Rov.(L) 09.75	10	0	1
York City 02.77	63	0	1
Halifax Town 04.78	75	1	0

IRELAND Simon P.

Barnstaple	23 November 1971		
Huddersfield Town 07.90	10	9	0
Wrexham 03.92	2	3	0
Blackburn Rovers 11.92	0	1	0
Mansfield Town 03.94	89	5	11
Doncaster Rov.(L) 10.96	9	0	1
Doncaster Rovers 01.97	52	0	1

IRVINE Alan J.

Glasgow	12 July 1958		
Everton 05.81	51	9	4
Crystal Palace 08.84	108	1	12
Blackburn Rovers 10.89	40	18	3

ISHERWOOD Roy E.

Blackburn	24 January 1934		
Blackburn Rovers 10.57	49	0	9

JACKSON Harry

Blackburn	30 December 1918		
Manchester City 06.46	8	0	2
Preston North End 12.47	18	0	5
Blackburn Rovers 12.48	1	0	0
Chester City 07.49	21	0	10

JANSEN Matthew B.

Carlisle	20 October 1977		
Carlisle United 01.96	26	16	10
Crystal Palace 02.98	23	3	10
Blackburn Rovers 01.99	26	13	7

JOHNROSE Leonard

Preston	29 November 1969		
Blackburn Rovers 06.88	20	22	11
PNE(L) 01.92	1	2	1
Hartlepool United 02.92	59	7	11
Bury 12.93	181	7	20
Burnley 02.99	9	3	1

JOHNSON Arthur

Liverpool	23 January 1933		
Blackburn Rovers 01.50	1	0	0
Halifax Town 03.55	216	0	0
Wrexham 06.60	52	0	0
Chester City 08.62	3	0	0

JOHNSON Damien M.

Lisburn	18 November 1978		
Blackburn Rovers 02.96	25	12	2
Notts Forest(L) 01.98	5	1	0

JOHNSTON Thomas B.

Loanhead	18 August 1927		
Darlington 04.51	27	0	9
Oldham Athletic 03.52	5	0	3
Norwich City 06.52	60	0	28
Newport County 10.54	63	0	46
Leyton Orient 02.56	87	0	70
Blackburn Rovers 03.58	36	0	21
Leyton Orient 02.59	93	0	51
Gillingham 09.61	35	0	10

JONES George A.

Radcliffe	21 April 1945		
Bury 06.62	63	0	14
Blackburn Rovers 03.64	36	3	14
Bury 11.66	249	7	100
Oldham Athletic 03.73	63	8	19
Halifax Town 02.76	18	1	4
Southport 01.77	54	1	11

JONES Robert W.

Liverpool — 28 March 1933

Club			
Southport 07.51	22	0	0
Chester City 08.53	166	0	0
Blackburn Rovers 03.58	49	0	0

JONES Roger

Upton-on-Severn — 8 November 1946

Club			
Bournemouth 05.65	160	0	0
Blackburn Rovers 01.70	242	0	0
Newcastle United 03.76	5	0	0
Stoke City 02.77	101	0	0
Derby County 07.80	59	0	0
Birmingham C.(L) 02.82	4	0	0
York City 08.82	122	0	0

JOYCE Walter

Oldham — 10 September 1937

Club			
Burnley 10.54	70	0	3
Blackburn Rovers 02.64	119	1	4
Oldham Athletic 09.67	68	3	2

KEELEY Glenn M.

Barking — 1 September 1954

Club			
Ipswich Town 08.72	4	0	0
Newcastle United 07.74	43	1	2
Blackburn Rovers 08.76	365	5	23
Everton(L) 10.82	1	0	0
Oldham Athletic 08.87	10	1	0
Colchester Utd(L) 02.88	4	0	0
Bolton Wanderers 09.88	20	0	0

KELLY Alan T.

Preston — 11 August 1968

Club			
Preston North End 09.85	142	0	0
Sheffield United 07.92	213	3	0
Blackburn Rovers 07.99	28	0	1

KELLY William M.

Cowdenbeath — 14 August 1922

Club			
Blackburn Rovers 09.51	186	0	1
Accrington Stanley 09.57	24	0	0

KENDALL Howard

Ryton-on-Tyne — 22 May 1946

Club			
Preston North End 05.63	104	0	13
Everton 03.67	227	2	21
Birmingham City 02.74	115	0	16
Stoke City 08.77	82	0	9
BlackburnRovers07.79	79	0	6
Everton(NC)08.81	4	0	0

KENNA Jeffrey J.

Dublin — 27 August 1970

Club			
Southampton 04.89	110	4	4
Blackburn Rovers 03.95	148	1	1

KENNEDY Andrew J.

Stirling — 8 October 1964

Club			
Birmingham City 03.85	51	25	19
Sheffield United(L) 03.87	8	1	1
Blackburn Rovers 06.88	49	10	23
Watford 08.90	17	8	4
Bolton W.(L) 10.91	1	0	0
Brighton & HA 09.92	34	8	10
Gillingham(NC) 09.94	0	2	0

KENNEDY Patrick A.

Dublin — 9 October 1934

Club			
ManchesterUnited 02.53	1	0	0
Blackburn Rovers 08.56	3	0	0
Southampton 07.59	2	0	0

KENYON John F.

Blackburn — 2 December 1953

Club			
BlackburnRovers 12.72	32	14	7

KERR James P.

Glasgow — 2 September 1949

Club			
Bury 09.66	150	2	37
Blackburn Rovers 05.70	11	0	0

KNIGHTON Kenneth

Darton — 20 February 1944

Club			
Wolverhampton W. 02.61	13	3	0
Oldham Athletic 11.66	45	0	4
Preston North End 11.67	62	0	3
Blackburn Rovers 06.69	70	0	11
Hull City 03.71	79	1	9
Sheffield Wed. 08.73	71	5	2

KOPEL Frank

Falkirk — 28 March 1949

Club			
Manchester United 04.66	8	2	0
Blackburn Rovers 03.69	23	2	0

LANGTON Robert

Ormskirk — 8 September 1918

Club			
Blackburn Rovers 09.38	107	0	24
Preston North End 08.48	55	0	14
Bolton Wanderers 11.49	118	0	16
Blackburn Rovers 09.53	105	0	33

LAWTHER Ian W.

Belfast — 20 October 1939

Club			
Sunderland 03.58	75	0	41
Blackburn Rovers 07.61	59	0	21
Scunthorpe United 07.63	60	0	22
Brentford 11.64	138	1	43
Halifax Town 08.68	87	14	23

Stockport County 07.71 158 6 29

LEAVER Derek
Blackburn 13 November 1930
Blackburn Rovers 05.49 14 0 5
Bournemouth 07.55 29 0 5
Crewe Alexandra 03.58 28 0 6

LE SAUX Graeme P.
Jersey 17 October 1968
Chelsea 12.87 77 13 8
Blackburn Rovers 03.93 127 2 7
Chelsea 08.97 56 1 1

LEWIS John F.
Long Eaton 22 March 1948
Lincoln City 03.67 47 15 9
Grimsby Town 01.70 23 127 74
Blackburn Rovers 08.77 24 4 6
Doncaster Rovers 08.78 48 16 10

LEYLAND Harry K.
Liverpool 12 May 1930
Everton 08.50 36 0 0
Blackburn Rovers 08.56 166 0 0
Tranmere Rovers 03.61 180 0 0

LIVINGSTONE Stephen C.
Middlesbrough 8 September 1968
Coventry City 07.86 17 14 5
Blackburn Rovers 01.91 25 5 10
Chelsea 03.93 0 1 0
Port Vale(L) 09.93 4 1 0
Grimsby Town 10.93 155 40 33

LORD Frank
Oldham 13 March 1936
Rochdale 10.53 122 0 54
Crewe Alexandra 07.61 108 0 68
Plymouth Argyle 11.63 69 1 23
Stockport County 02.66 27 0 18
Blackburn Rovers 12.66 10 0 1
Chesterfield 06.67 12 0 6
Plymouth Argyle 10.67 6 0 2

LOWEY John A.
Manchester 7 March 1958
Sheffield Wed. 10.78 35 7 4
Blackburn Rovers 11.80 136 5 14
Wigan Athletic 07.86 1 2 0
Chesterfield(L) 11.86 2 0 0
York City(L) 03.87 3 3 0
Preston North End 08.87 4 0 1
Chester City 03.88 9 0 0

McATEER Jason W.
Birkenhead 18 June 1971
Bolton Wanderers 01.92 109 5 8
Liverpool 09.95 84 16 3
Blackburn Rovers 01.99 34 4 3

McCAIG Robert A.M.
Lockerbie 15 August 1923
Carlisle United 08.48 5 0 0
Blackburn Rovers 12.48 30 0 2
Stockport County 08.51 15 0 2
Halifax Town 01.52 17 0 2
Crewe Alexandra 08.52 19 0 1

McCLELLAND Charles
Lochgelly 8 January 1924
Blackburn Rovers 12.46 13 0 2
Exeter City 07.49 183 0 60

McDONALD Gerard
Milnthorpe 3 December 1952
Blackburn Rovers 12.70 19 2 2
Halifax Town 08.73 10 3 0

McEVOY Andrew M.
Dublin 15 July 1938
Blackburn Rovers 10.56 183 0 89

McGORRIGHAN Francis O.
Easington 20 November 1921
Hull City 08.46 20 0 1
Blackburn Rovers 02.47 5 0 0
Hull City 09.47 6 0 0
Southport 08.48 4 0 0

McGRATH Michael
Dublin 7 April 1936
Blackburn Rovers 08.54 268 0 8
Bradford PA 03.66 50 0 2

McKEE William A.
Warrington 6 June 1928
Blackburn Rovers 11.49 1 0 0

McKENZIE Duncan
Grimsby 10 June 1950
Nottingham Forest 07.68 105 6 41
Mansfield Town(L) 03.70 7 3 3
Mansfield Town(L) 02.73 6 0 7
Leeds United 08.74 64 2 27
Everton 12.76 48 0 14
Chelsea 08.78 15 0 4
Blackburn Rovers 03.79 74 0 16

McKINLAY William

Glasgow	22 April 1969		
Blackburn Rovers 10.95	76	4	3

McKINNON Paul J.

Frimley	1 August 1958		
Blackburn Rovers 12.86	5	0	0

McLEAN William

Liverpool	14 August 1931		
Blackburn Rovers 02.53	12	0	0

MacLEOD Alistair R.

Glasgow	1 January 1951		
Blackburn Rovers 06.56	193	0	47

MacLUCKIE George R.

Falkirk	19 September 1931		
Blackburn Rovers 08.52	20	0	2
Ipswich Town 05.53	141	0	24
Reading 06.58	85	0	8

McNAMEE John

Coatbridge	11 June 1941		
Newcastle United 12.66	115	2	8
Blackburn Rovers 11.71	56	0	9
Hartlepool United 12.73	2	0	0
Workington(NC) 08.75	2	0	0

MAIL David

Bristol	12 September 1962		
Blackburn Rovers 01.82	200	6	4
HullCity 07.90	140	10	2

MAKEL Lee R.

Sunderland	11 January 1973		
Newcastle United 02.91	6	6	1
Blackburn Rovers 07.92	1	5	0
Huddersfield Town 10.95	62	3	5

MARCOLIN Dario

Brescia,Italy	28 October 1971		
Blackburn Rov.(L) 10.98	5	5	1

MARKER Nicholas R.T.

BudleighSalterton	3 May 1965		
Exeter City 05.83	196	6	3
Plymouth Argyle 10.87	201	1	13
Blackburn Rovers 09.92	41	13	1
Sheffield United 07.97	60	1	5
Plymouth A.(L) 02.99	4	0	0

MARKS George W.

Amesbury	9 April 1915		
Arsenal 03.36	2	0	0
Blackburn Rovers 08.46	67	0	0
Bristol City 08.48	9	0	0
Reading 10.48	118	0	0

MARRIOTT Andrew

Sutton-in-Ashfield	11 October 1970		
Nottingham Forest 06.89	11	0	0
WBA(L) 09.89	3	0	0
BlackburnRov.(L) 12.89	2	0	0
Colchester Utd.(L) 03.90	10	0	0
Burnley(L) 08.91	15	0	0
Wrexham 10.93	213	0	0
Sunderland 08.98	1	0	0

MARTIN Donald

Corby	15 February 1944		
Northampton T. 07.62	136	0	53
Blackburn Rovers 02.68	218	6	58
Northampton T. 11.75	77	15	17

MAY David

Oldham	24 June 1970		
Blackburn Rovers 06.88	123	0	3
Manchester United 07.94	65	14	6

METCALFE Stuart M.

Blackburn	6 October 1950		
Blackburn Rovers 01.68	375	11	21
Carlisle United 07.80	23	2	3
Blackburn R.(NC) 10.82	1	0	0
Crewe Alex.(NC) 01.83	3	0	0

MILLAR John

Coatbridge	8 December 1966		
Chelsea 08.84	11	0	0
Northampton T.(L) 01.87	1	0	0
Blackburn Rovers 07.87	122	4	2

MILLER Alan J.

Epping	29 March 1970		
Arsenal 05.88	6	2	0
Plymouth A.(L) 11.88	13	0	0
WBA(L) 08.91	3	0	0
Birmingham C.(L) 12.91	15	0	0
Middlesbrough 08.94	57	0	0
Grimsby Town(L) 01.97	3	0	0
WBA 02.97	73	0	0
Blackburn Rovers 07.99	1	0	0

MILLER Ian

Perth	13 May 1955		
Bury 08.73	9	6	0

NottinghamForest 08.74	0	0	0
Doncaster Rovers 08.75	124	0	14
Swindon Town 07.78	123	4	9
Blackburn Rovers 08.81	252	16	16
Port Vale 07.89	14	7	1
Scunthorpe United 08.90	8	4	0

MIMMS Robert A.

York	12 October 1963		
Rotherham United 11.81	83	0	0
Everton 06.85	29	0	0
Notts County(L) 03.86	2	0	0
Sunderland(L) 12.86	4	0	0
Blackburn Rov.(L) 01.87	6	0	0
Manchester City(L) 09.87	3	0	0
Tottenham H. 02.88	37	0	0
Blackburn Rovers 12.90	126	2	0
Crystal Palace(NC) 08.96	1	0	0
Preston North End 09.96	27	0	0
Rotherham United 08.97	43	0	0
York City 08.98	35	0	0

MITCHELL Albert J.

Burslem	22 January 1922		
Stoke City 05.41	10	0	2
Blackburn Rovers 02.48	3	0	0
Northampton T. 05.49	81	0	21
Luton Town 07.51	106	0	41
Middlesbrough 09.54	50	0	6
Southport 08.56	16	0	3

MITCHELL Robert

SouthShields	4 January 1955		
Sunderland 01.72	1	2	0
Blackburn Rovers 07.76	17	12	6
Grimsby Town 06.78	142	0	6
Carlisle United 08.82	2	0	0
Rotherham United 03.83	86	9	2
Lincoln City 01.86	41	3	2

MOONEY Francis

Fauldhouse	1 January 1932		
BlackburnRovers 02.54	58	0	19
Carlisle United 05.56	124	0	24

MOORE Norman W.

Grimsby	15 October 1919		
Grimsby Town 03.39	7	0	1
Hull City 04.47	81	0	46
Blackburn Rovers 03.50	7	0	1
Bury 08.51	2	0	0

MORAN Kevin B.

Dublin	29 April 1956		
Manchester United 02.78	228	3	21
Blackburn Rovers 01.90	143	4	10

MORLEY Brian J.

Fleetwood	4 October 1960		
BlackburnRovers 10.78	20	0	0
Tranmere Rovers 08.81	10	6	2

MORRIS Peter A.

Farnworth	23 November 1958		
Blackburn Rovers 07.78	2	2	0

MORRISON Andrew C.

Inverness	30 July 1970		
Plymouth Argyle 07.88	105	8	6
Blackburn Rovers 08.93	1	4	0
Blackpool 12.94	47	0	3
Huddersfield Town 07.96	43	2	2
Manchester City 10.98	21	1	4

MULLEN James

Oxford	16 March 1947		
Reading 11.66	8	0	1
Charlton Athletic 11.67	7	0	0
Rotherham United 02.69	174	3	24
Blackburn Rovers 08.74	6	4	0
Bury 06.76	2	2	0
Rochdale(L) 03.77	6	2	1

MULVANEY Richard

Sunderland	5 August 1942		
Blackburn Rovers 02.64	135	6	4
Oldham Athletic 08.71	88	4	2
Rochdale 10.74	72	1	4

MUNRO Stuart

Falkirk	15 September 1962		
Blackburn Rovers 07.91	1	0	0
Bristol City 02.93	91	3	0

MURPHY Donal P.

Dublin	23 February 1955		
Coventry City 08.72	33	10	10
Millwall(L) 10.77	3	0	0
Torquay United 05.78	81	4	20
Plymouth Argyle 06.80	44	4	9
Torquay United(L) 12.81	2	1	0
Blackburn Rovers 02.82	1	2	0

MURPHY Edwin T.

Middlesbrough	5 March 1921		
Middlesbrough 05.39	9	0	1
Blackburn Rovers 12.47	31	0	6
Halifax Town 03.49	217	0	30

113

NAPIER Christopher R.A.

Dunblane	26 September 1943		
Blackpool 11.60	2	0	0
Preston North End 06.63	1	0	0
Workington 07.64	58	0	25
Newcastle United 11.65	8	0	0
Brighton & HA 09.66	249	7	84
Blackburn Rovers 08.72	53	1	10

NEEDHAM Andrew P.

Oldham	13 September 1955		
Birmingham City 08.73	2	1	1
Blackburn Rovers 07.76	4	1	0
Aldershot 03.77	92	3	29

NEWELL Michael C.

Liverpool	27 January 1965		
Crewe Alexandra 09.83	3	0	0
Wigan Athletic 10.83	64	8	25
Luton Town 01.86	62	1	18
Leicester City 09.87	81	0	21
Everton 06.89	48	20	15
Blackburn Rovers 11.91	113	17	28
Birmingham City 07.96	11	4	1
West Ham Utd.(L) 12.96	6	1	0
Bradford City(L) 03.97	7	0	0
Crewe Alexandra 03.99	1	3	0

NEWTON Keith R.

Manchester	23 June 1941		
Blackburn Rovers 10.58	306	0	9
Everton 12.69	48	1	1
Burnley 06.72	209	0	5

NIGHTINGALE Albert

Rotherham	10 November 1923		
Sheffield United 06.41	62	0	14
Huddersfield Town 03.48	119	0	20
Blackburn Rovers 10.51	35	0	5
Leeds United 10.52	130	0	48

OAKES John

Hamilton	6 December 1919		
Blackburn Rovers 02.47	35	0	9
Manchester City 06.48	77	0	9

OATES Graham

Bradford	14 March 1949		
Bradford City 02.70	158	3	19
Blackburn Rovers 06.74	76	0	10
Newcastle United 03.76	26	9	3

O'KEEFE Vincent J.

Birmingham	2 April 1957		
Exeter City 06.78	53	0	0

Torquay United 02.80	108	0	0
Blackburn Rovers 08.82	68	0	0
Bury(L) 10.83	2	0	0
Blackpool(L) 12.86	1	0	0
Blackpool(L) 02.89	6	0	0
Wrexham 07.89	83	0	0
Exeter City(NC) 08.92	2	0	0

O'LEARY Donal P.

Limehouse	24 June 1936		
Blackburn Rovers 10.54	6	0	1

OLIVER Neil

Berwick	11 April 1967		
Blackburn Rovers 08.89	5	1	0

O'MARA John

Farnworth	19 March 1947		
Brentford 03.71	53	0	28
Blackburn Rovers 09.72	30	5	10
Bradford City 12.74	3	0	1

OSTENSTAD Egil

Haugesun, Norway	2 January 1972		
Southampton 10.96	77	16	28
Blackburn Rovers 07.99	21	7	8

PARKER Harry

Blackburn	8 February 1933		
Blackburn Rovers 08.51	3	0	0

PARKER Stuart J.

Preston	16 February 1954		
Blackpool 04.72	10	6	2
SouthendUnited 07.75	62	2	23
Chesterfield 02.77	30	4	8
Blackburn Rovers 07.79	5	4	1
Bury 09.82	26	8	9
Chester City(NC) 09.83	9	0	5
Stockport Co.(NC) 02.84	0	1	0

PARKES Tony

Sheffield	5 May 1949		
Blackburn Rovers 05.70	345	5	38

PARKIN Timothy J.

Penrith	31 December 1957		
Blackburn Rovers 03.76	13	0	0
Bristol Rovers 08.81	205	1	12
SwindonTown 07.86	109	1	6
PortVale 12.89	41	7	1
Shrewsbury T.(L) 09.91	5	0	0
Darlington 08.92	40	0	2

PATTERSON John G.

Cramlington	6 July 1922		
Blackburn Rovers 04.45	107	0	0

PATTERSON Mark A.

Darwen	24 May 1965		
Blackburn Rovers 05.83	89	12	20
Preston North End 06.88	54	1	19
Bury 02.90	42	0	10
Bolton Wanderers 01.91	158	11	11
Sheffield United 12.95	72	2	4
Southend Utd.(L) 03.97	4	0	0
Bury 12.97	27	4	2
Blackpool(L) 12.98	7	0	0
Southend United 03.99	5	0	0

PEACOCK Darren

Bristol	3 February 1968		
Newport County 02.86	24	4	0
Hereford United 03.89	56	3	4
QPR 12.90	123	3	6
Newcastle United 03.94	131	2	2
Blackburn Rovers 07.98	42	5	1

PEARCE Ian A.

BuryStEdmunds	7 May 1974		
Chelsea 08.91	0	4	0
Blackburn Rovers 10.93	43	19	2
West Ham United 09.97	63	0	3

PEDERSEN Per W.

Denmark	30 March 1969		
Blackburn Rovers 02.97	6	5	1

PEDERSEN Tore

Norway	29 September 1969		
Oldham Athletic 10.93	7	3	0
Blackburn Rovers 09.97	3	2	0

PEREZ Sebastian

StChamond, France	24 November 1973		
Blackburn Rovers 07.98	4	1	1

PICKERING Frederick

Blackburn	19 January 1941		
Blackburn Rovers 01.58	123	0	59
Everton 03.64	97	0	56
Birmingham City 08.67	74	0	27
Blackpool 06.69	48	1	24
Blackburn Rovers 03.71	11	0	2

PRICE Christopher J.

Hereford	30 March 1960		
Hereford United 01.78	327	3	27

Blackburn Rovers 07.86	83	0	11
Aston Villa 05.88	109	2	2
Blackburn Rovers 02.92	13	6	3
Portsmouth 01.93	14	4	0

PRICE John

Easington	25 October 1943		
Burnley 11.60	21	0	2
Stockport County 05.65	241	5	23
Blackburn Rovers 09.71	63	13	12
Stockport County 03.74	51	15	1

PRIDAY Robert H.

SouthAfrica	29 March 1925		
Liverpool 12.45	33	0	6
Blackburn Rovers 03.49	44	0	11
Accrington Stanley 12.52	5	0	0
Rochdale 08.53	5	0	1

PRYDE Robert

Wemyss	25 April 1913		
Blackburn Rovers 05.33	320	0	11

QUIGLEY Edward

Bury	13 July 1921		
Bury 09.41	42	0	18
Sheffield Wed. 10.47	74	0	49
Preston North End 12.49	52	0	17
Blackburn Rovers 11.51	159	0	92
Bury 08.56	10	0	3

QUINN Desmond

Derry	21 March 1926		
Blackburn Rovers 08.47	1	0	0
Millwall 06.49	43	0	0

QUINN James M.

Belfast	18 November 1959		
Swindon Town 12.81	34	15	10
Blackburn Rovers 08.84	58	13	17
Swindon Town 12.86	61	3	30
Leicester City 06.88	131	8	6
Bradford City 03.89	35	0	14
West Ham United 12.89	34	13	19
Bournemouth 08.91	43	0	19
Reading 07.92	149	33	71
Peterborough Utd. 07.97	47	2	25

RADFORD John

Hemsworth	22 February 1947		
Arsenal 03.64	375	4	111
West Ham United 12.76	28	0	0
Blackburn Rovers 02.78	36	0	10

The Blue and Whites

RAMSBOTTOM Neil
Blackburn   25 February 1946

Club	App		Goals
Bury 07.64	174	0	0
Blackpool 02.71	13	0	0
Crewe Alex.(L) 01.72	3	0	0
Coventry City 03.72	51	0	0
Sheffield Wed. 08.75	18	0	0
Plymouth Argyle 07.76	39	0	0
Blackburn Rovers 01.78	10	0	0
Sheffield United 10.79	2	0	0
Bradford City 08.80	73	0	0
Bournemouth(NC) 08.83	4	0	0

RANDELL Colin W.
Neath   12 December 1952

Club	App		Goals
Plymouth Argyle 09.73	137	2	9
Exeter City 09.77	78	0	4
Plymouth Argyle 07.79	110	0	8
Blackburn Rovers 08.82	72	1	7
Newport Co.(L) 03.84	15	0	0
Swansea City 07.85	20	2	1

RATCLIFFE Barrie J.
Blackburn   21 September 1941

Club	App		Goals
Blackburn Rovers 09.58	36	0	4
Scunthorpe United 05.64	26	0	7
Rochdale 07.65	12	0	1

RATHBONE Michael J
Birmingham   6 November 1958

Club	App		Goals
Birmingham City 11.76	17	3	0
Blackburn Rovers 03.79	270	3	2
Preston North End 07.87	82	9	4

REEVES Brian T.
Skelmersdale   18 February 1939

Club	App		Goals
Blackburn Rovers 08.60	12	0	0
Scunthorpe United 04.62	38	0	0
Southport 07.65	143	0	0

REID NIcholas S.
Urmston   30 October 1960

Club	App		Goals
Manchester City 10.78	211	5	2
Blackburn Rovers 07.87	160	14	9
Bristol City(L) 09.92	3	1	0
WBA 11.92	13	7	0
Wycombe W. 03.94	6	2	0
Bury 12.95	19	6	0

RICHARDSON Lee J.
Halifax   12 March 1969

Club	App		Goals
Halifax Town 07.87	43	13	2
Watford 02.89	40	1	1
Blackburn Rovers 08.90	50	12	3
Oldham Athletic 08.94	82	6	1
Stockport Co.(L) 08.97	4	2	0
Huddersfield Town 10.97	29	7	3

RIPLEY Stuart E.
Middlesbrough   20 November 1967

Club	App		Goals
Middlesbrough 12.85	210	39	26
Bolton W.(L) 02.86	5	0	1
Blackburn Rovers 07.92	172	15	13
Southampton 07.98	16	6	0

ROBERTS John T.
Australia   24 March 1944

Club	App		Goals
Blackburn Rovers 04.66	3	0	0
Chesterfield 08.67	46	0	0
Bradford City 08.68	44	0	0
Southend United 01.71	47	0	0
Northampton T. 07.72	13	0	0

ROBERTS Thomas
Liverpool   28 July 1927

Club	App		Goals
Blackburn Rovers 12.51	6	0	0
Watford 12.54	1	0	0
Chester City 02.56	5	0	0

ROGERS Eamonn E.
Dublin   16 April 1947

Club	App		Goals
Blackburn Rovers 05.65	159	6	30
Charlton Athletic 10.71	37	2	3
Northampton T.(L) 11.72	4	0	1

ROGERS William
Ulverston   3 July 1919

Club	App		Goals
Blackburn Rovers 06.38	73	0	24
Barrow 10.47	197	0	14

ROUND Paul G.
Blackburn   22 June 1959

Club	App		Goals
Blackburn Rovers 08.77	41	10	5

RUSSELL Alexander
Seaham   21 February 1944

Club	App		Goals
Southport 11.63	262	1	63
BlackburnRovers08.70	22	2	4
TranmereRovers07.71	54	1	7
CreweAlex.(L)10.72	4	0	0
Southport11.72	84	1	12

SALMON Michael B.
Leyland   14 July 1964

Club	App		Goals
Blackburn Rovers 10.81	1	0	0
Chester City(L) 10.82	16	0	0
Stockport County 08.83	118	0	0
Bolton Wanderers 07.86	26	0	0
Wrexham 03.87	100	0	0
Charlton Athletic 07.89	148	0	0

116

SELLARS Scott

Sheffield	27 November 1965		
Leeds United 07.83	72	4	12
Blackburn Rovers 07.86	194	8	35
Leeds United 07.92	6	1	0
Newcastle United 03.93	56	5	5
Bolton Wanderers 12.95	106	5	15

SHANAHAN Terence C.

Paddington	5 December 1951		
Ipswich Town 07.69	3	1	0
Blackburn Rov.(L) 09.71	6	0	2
Halifax Town 11.71	88	8	23
Chesterfield 10.74	56	4	28
Millwall 04.76	13	7	5
Bournemouth 07.77	14	4	1
Aldershot 07.78	16	0	4

SHARPLES George F.V.

Ellesmere Port	20 September 1943		
Everton 09.60	10	0	0
Blackburn Rovers 03.65	99	4	5
Southport 07.71	23	2	0

SHEARER Alan

Newcastle	13 August 1970		
Southampton 04.88	105	13	23
Blackburn Rovers 07.92	132	6	112
Newcastle United 07.96	111	4	64

SHEARER Duncan N.

Fort William	28 August 1962		
Chelsea 11.83	2	0	1
Huddersfield Town 03.86	80	3	38
Swindon Town 06.88	156	3	78
Blackburn Rovers 03.92	5	1	1

SHEPSTONE Paul T.A.

Coventry	8 November 1970		
Blackburn Rovers 05.90	16	10	1
York City(L) 03.92	2	0	0

SHORT Craig J.

Bridlington	25 June 1968		
Scarborough 10.87	61	2	7
Notts County 07.89	128	0	6
Derby County 09.92	118	0	9
Everton 07.95	90	9	4
Blackburn Rovers 07.99	17	0	0

SILVESTER Peter D.

Wokingham	19 February 1948		
Reading 02.66	76	3	26
Norwich City 09.69	99	1	37

Colchester Utd.(L) 10.73	4	0	0
Southend United 02.74	79	2	32
Reading(L) 03.75	2	0	0
Blackburn Rov.(L)10.76	5	0	1
Cambridge United 08.77	2	2	1

SIMS Christopher H.

Liverpool	6 December 1939		
Blackburn Rovers 04.59	13	0	0

SKINNER Craig R.

Heywood	21 October 1970		
Blackburn Rovers 06.89	11	5	0
Plymouth Argyle 08.92	42	11	4
Wrexham 07.95	70	17	10
York City 03.99	3	2	0

SLATER Robert D.

Ormskirk	22 November 1964		
Blackburn Rovers 08.94	12	6	0
West Ham United 08.95	18	7	2
Southampton 09.96	25	16	2
WolverhamptonW. 03.98	4	2	0

SMITH John

Batley	17 February 1915		
Huddersfield Town 06.32	45	0	24
Newcastle United 09.34	104	0	69
Manchester United 02.38	36	0	14
Blackburn Rovers 03.46	30	0	12
Port Vale 05.47	29	0	10

SMITH William H.

Plymouth	7 September 1926		
Reading 08.47	3	0	0
Northampton T. 07.48	26	0	6
Birmingham City 02.50	55	0	21
Blackburn Rovers 12.52	119	0	10
Accrington Stanley 07.60	34	0	3

SPEEDIE David R.

Glenrothes	20 February 1960		
Barnsley 10.78	10	13	0
Darlington 06.80	88	0	21
Chelsea 06.82	155	7	47
Coventry City 07.87	121	1	31
Liverpool 02.91	8	4	6
Blackburn Rovers 08.91	34	2	23
Southampton 07.92	11	0	0
Birmingham C.(L) 10.92	10	0	2
WBA(L) 01.93	7	0	2
West Ham Utd.(L) 03.93	11	0	4
Leicester City 07.93	37	0	12

SPEIGHT Michael
Upton	1 November 1951		
Sheffield United 05.69	184	15	14
Blackburn Rovers 07.80	50	1	4
Grimsby Town 08.82	35	3	2
Chester City 08.84	40	0	1

STAPLETON Francis A.
Dublin	10 July 1956		
Arsenal 09.73	223	2	75
Manchester United 08.81	204	19	60
Derby County 03.88	10	0	1
Blackburn Rovers 07.89	80	1	13
H'sfield T.(NC) 10.91	5	0	0
Bradford City 12.91	49	19	2
Brighton & HA 11.94	1	1	0

STARBUCK Philip M.
Nottingham	24 November 1968		
Nottingham Forest 08.86	9	27	2
Birmingham C.(L) 03.88	3	0	0
Hereford Utd.(L) 02.90	6	0	0
Blackburn Rov.(L) 09.90	5	1	1
Huddersfield Town 08.91	120	17	36
Sheffield United 10.94	26	10	2
Bristol City(L) 09.95	5	0	1
Oldham Athletic 08.97	7	2	1
Plymouth Argyle 03.98	6	1	0

STEPHAN Harold W.
Farnworth	24 February 1924		
Blackburn Rovers 09.44	13	0	1

STEPHENSON Roy
Crook	27 May 1932		
Burnley 06.49	78	0	27
Rotherham United 09.56	43	0	14
Blackburn Rovers 11.57	21	0	5
Leicester City 03.59	12	0	0
Ipswich Town 07.60	144	0	21

STONEHOUSE Kevin
BishopAuckland	20 September 1959		
Blackburn Rovers 07.79	77	8	27
Huddersfield Town 03.83	20	2	4
Blackpool 03.84	53	2	19
Darlington 07.87	59	13	20
Carlisle United(L) 03.89	0	3	0
Rochdale 07.89	13	1	2

SUART Ronald
Kendal	18 November 1920		
Blackpool 01.39	104	0	0
Blackburn Rovers 09.49	176	0	0

SULLEY Christophe r S.
Camberwell	3 December 1959		
Bournemouth 03.81	205	1	3
Blackburn Rovers 03.87	134	0	3
Port Vale 07.92	40	0	1
Preston North End 07.93	21	0	1

SUTTON Christopher R.
Nottingham	10 March 1973		
Norwich City 07.91	89	13	35
Blackburn Rovers 07.94	125	5	47

SVARC Robert L.
Leicester	8 February 1946		
Leicester City 03.63	13	0	2
Lincoln City 12.68	40	5	16
Barrow(L) 09.70	15	0	3
Colchester United 12.72	116	0	59
Blackburn Rovers 10.75	42	8	16
Watford(L) 09.77	1	0	0

SWINDELLS Jack
Manchester	12 April 1937		
Blackburn Rovers 11.57	9	0	1
Accrington Stanley 12.59	65	0	28
Barnsley 06.61	14	0	8
Workington 02.62	61	0	19
Torquay United 07.63	18	0	6
Newport County 07.64	23	0	3

TAYLOR Gordon
Ashton-under-Lyne	28 December 1944		
BoltonWanderers 01.62	253	6	41
Birmingham City 12.70	156	10	9
Blackburn Rovers 03.76	62	2	3
Bury 06.78	58	2	2

TAYLOR Kenneth G.
SouthShields	15 March 1931		
Blackburn Rovers 01.50	200	0	0

TAYLOR Martin
Ashington	9 November 1979		
Blackburn Rovers 08.97	5	4	0

TAYLOR Royston
Blackpool	28 September 1956		
Preston North End 10.74	3	0	0
Blackburn Rovers 11.76	3	0	1

THOMAS Edward
Newton-le-Willows	23 October 1933		
Everton 10.51	86	0	39
Blackburn Rovers 02.60	37	0	9

Swansea City 07.62	68	0	21
Derby County 08.64	102	3	43
Leyton Orient 09.67	11	0	2

THOMPSON Christopher D.

Walsall	24 January 1960		
Bolton Wanderers 07.77	66	7	18
Lincoln City(L) 03.83	5	1	0
Blackburn Rovers 08.83	81	4	24
WiganAthletic 07.86	67	7	12
Blackpool 07.88	27	12	8
Cardiff City 03.90	1	1	0
Walsall(NC) 02.91	3	0	0

THORLEY Dennis

Stoke	7 November 1956		
Stoke City 07.76	9	4	0
Blackburn Rovers 03.80	2	2	0

TODD Paul R.

Middlesbrough	8 May 1920		
Doncaster Rovers 09.45	160	0	51
Blackburn Rovers 07.50	46	0	12
Hull City 10.51	27	0	3

TOMLINSON Robert W.

Blackburn	4 June 1924		
Blackburn Rovers 01.43	25	0	0
Halifax Town 06.51	9	0	0

TURNER David J.

Retford	7 September 1943		
Newcastle United 10.60	2	0	0
Brighton & HA 12.63	292	8	30
Blackburn Rovers 08.72	23	2	0

VALERY Patrick J.C.

Brignoles, France	3 July 1969		
Blackburn Rovers 07.97	14	1	0

VENTERS Alexander

Cowdenbeath	9 June 1913		
Blackburn Rovers 02.47	25	0	7

VERNON Royston T.

Prestatyn	14 April 1937		
Blackburn Rovers 03.55	131	0	49
Everton 02.60	176	0	101
Stoke City 03.65	84	3	22
Halifax Town(L) 01.70	4	0	0

WADDINGTON John

Darwen	16 February 1952		
Blackburn Rovers 08.73	139	9	18

Bury 08.79	46	1	0

WAGSTAFFE David

Manchester	5 April 1943		
Manchester City 05.60	144	0	8
Wolverhampton W. 12.64	324	0	26
Blackburn Rovers 01.76	72	3	7
Blackpool 08.78	17	2	1
Blackburn Rovers 03.79	2	0	0

WARD Ashley S.

Manchester	24 November 1970		
Manchester City 08.89	0	1	0
Wrexham(L) 01.91	4	0	2
Leicester City 07.91	2	8	0
Blackpool(L) 11.92	2	0	1
Crewe Alexandra 12.92	58	3	25
Norwich City 12.94	53	0	18
Derby County 03.96	32	8	9
Barnsley 09.97	45	1	20
BlackburnRovers 12.98	50	2	13

WARHURST Paul

Stockport	26 September 1969		
Oldham Athletic 10.88	60	7	2
Sheffield Wed. 07.91	60	6	6
BlackburnRovers08.93	30	27	4
CrystalPalace07.97	27	0	4
BoltonWanderers11.98	17	3	0

WEBBER John V.

Blackpool	2 June 1918		
Blackburn Rovers 02.47	8	0	1

WEGERLE Roy C.

SouthAfrica	19 March 1964		
Chelsea 06.86	15	8	3
Swindon Town(L) 03.88	7	0	1
Luton Town 07.88	39	6	10
QPR 12.89	71	4	29
Blackburn Rovers 03.92	20	14	6
Coventry City 03.93	46	7	9

WEIR John B.

Fauldhouse	20 October 1923		
Blackburn Rovers 01.47	23	0	7

WESTCOTT Dennis

Wallasey	2 July 1917		
New Brighton 01.36	18	0	10
Wolverhampton W. 07.36	128	0	125
Blackburn Rovers 04.48	63	0	37
Manchester City 02.50	72	0	37
Chesterfield 06.52	40	0	21

119

WHALLEY Jeffrey H.

Rossendale	8 February 1952		
Blackburn Rovers 02.70	2	0	0

WHARTON John E.

Bolton	18 June 1920		
Plymouth Argyle 06.37	11	0	2
Preston North End 07.39	25	0	7
Manchester City 03.47	23	0	2
Blackburn Rovers 06.48	129	0	14
Newport County 02.53	74	0	10

WHEELER Alfred J.

Fareham	6 April 1922		
Blackburn Rovers 04.47	21	0	5
Swindon Town 07.49	23	0	4

WHELAN David

Bradford	24 November 1936		
Blackburn Rovers 12.53	78	0	3
Crewe Alexandra 01.63	115	0	0

WHITESIDE Arnold

Garstang	6 November 1933		
Blackburn Rovers 01.53	218	0	3

WHITTLE Maurice

Wigan	15 July 1948		
Blackburn Rovers 07.66	5	2	0
Oldham Athletic 05.69	307	5	39
Wigan Athletic 03.80	21	0	1

WIGHTMAN John R.

Duns	2 November 1912		
York City 08.33	5	0	0
Bradford PA 09.34	17	0	0
Huddersfield Town 01.35	64	0	0
Blackburn Rovers 01.37	66	0	2
Carlisle United 08.47	36	0	0

WILCOX Jason M.

Farnworth	15 July 1971		
Blackburn Rovers 06.89	243	25	31

WILKINSON David

Sunderland	28 May 1928		
Blackburn Rovers 07.48	1	0	0
Bournemouth 06.50	8	0	3

WILKINSON Neil

Blackburn	16 February 1955		
Blackburn Rovers 02.73	27	3	0
Port Vale 07.78	?	0	0
Crewe Alexandra 10.78	68	7	0

WILLIAMSON John

Manchester	8 May 1929		
Manchester City 08.49	59	0	18
Blackburn Rovers 03.56	9	0	3

WILLIAMSON Philip J.

Macclesfield	19 September 1962		
Blackburn Rovers 09.80	0	1	0

WILLIS John J.

Boldon	28 May 1934		
Blackburn Rovers 08.54	1	0	0
Aston Villa 08.58	1	0	0

WILSON William

Seaton Delaval	10 July 1946		
Blackburn Rovers 09.63	246	1	0
Portsmouth 01.72	187	6	5

WITSCHGE Richard

Netherlands	20 September 1969		
Blackburn Rov.(L) 03.95	1	0	0

WOOD Michael J.

Bury	3 July 1952		
Blackburn Rovers 02.70	140	8	2
Bradford City 02.78	143	3	9
Halifax Town 08.82	80	1	2

WOODS Maurice

Skelmersdale	1 November 1931		
Everton 11.49	8	0	1
Blackburn Rovers 11.56	260	0	2
Luton Town 07.65	34	0	0
Stockport County 07.66	85	0	2

WRIGHT Alan G.

Ashton-under-Lyne	28 September 1971		
Blackpool 04.89	91	7	0
Blackburn Rovers 10.91	67	7	1
Aston Villa 03.95	157	2	3

WRIGHT Archibald W.

Glasgow	23 November 1924		
Blackburn Rovers 05.51	22	0	10
Grimsby Town 07.53	39	0	9
Accrington Stanley 06.54	80	0	27

WRIGHT Glenn

Liverpool	26 May 1956		
Blackburn Rovers 12.73	1	0	0